The Super Reader Protocol: The Guided Reading & Reading Comprehension Blueprint

How Every Adult Reader Can Improve Reading Fluency in 3 weeks or less. (Without The Embarrassment & Stuttering!)

Author: Dr. Herman Kynaston

© Copyright 2020 - All rights reserved.

The content contained within this book may not be reproduced, duplicated or transmitted without direct written permission from the author or the publisher.

Under no circumstances will any blame or legal responsibility be held against the publisher, or author, for any damages, reparation, or monetary loss due to the information contained within this book, either directly or indirectly.

Legal Notice:

This book is copyright protected. It is only for personal use. You cannot amend, distribute, sell, use, quote or paraphrase any part, or the content within this book,

Disclaimer Notice:

Please note the information contained within this document is for educational and entertainment purposes only. All effort has been executed to present accurate, up to date, reliable, complete information. No warranties of any kind are declared or implied. Readers acknowledge that the author is not engaging in the rendering of legal, financial, medical or professional advice. The content within this book has been derived from various sources. Please consult a licensed professional before attempting any techniques outlined in this book.

By reading this document, the reader agrees that under no circumstances is the author responsible for any losses, direct or indirect, that are incurred as a result of the use of information contained within this document, including, but not limited to, errors, omissions, or inaccuracies.

Free Gift

This book includes a bonus booklet. This giveaway may be for a limited time only. All information on how you can secure your gift right now can be found at the end of this book.

Table Of Contents

BOOK DESCRIPTION: 3
INTRODUCTION 6
CHAPTER 1 GUIDED READING IN THE CLASSROOM 9
   The Importance of Guided Reading 9
   Encouraging Independence 10
      Independent literacy activities *12*
   Guided Reading Process 13
   Additional Guided Reading Tips 14
CHAPTER 2 GUIDED READING 16
   Guided Reading Process 16
   Assess 16
   Decide 18
   Guide 24
      Use assessments to plan and teach *24*
      Reading, word study, writing *31*
   Tools To Help With Monitoring and Assessing Students 32
      Sample Observation Sheet *32*
   How To Keep Your Groups and Students Organized 33
CHAPTER 3 GUIDED READING LEVELS 36
   What the Reading Levels Mean 36
   Overview of Reading Levels 37
   Leveled Literacy Intervention 40

Guided Reading Categories 42
Getting Started Tips 45

CHAPTER 4 PRE-K (LEVEL PRE-A) 48

Guided Reading for Non-readers 48
- *Teaching points and strategies* 49

Letter Recognition Strategies 50
- *Letter Sorting by Shape* 50
- *Letter Hunt* 51
- *Alphabet Book* 51
- *Letter Activities* 51

Sound Recognition Strategies 52
- *Picture Activities* 52
- *Letter Hunt Using Words* 53

Ways To Include Reading With Nonreaders 53
- *Shared reading* 54
- *Echo reading* 54
- *Choral reading* 54
- *Read out loud* 54

Letter Knowledge 55
- *Memory Game* 55
- *Word Building* 55

Introducing Sight Words or High-frequency Words 55
- *Word search* 56
- *Building words activities* 56

Introducing Phonemic Awareness 56
- *Using word families* 57
- *Identify sound in words* 58

Things To Keep in Mind 58

CHAPTER 5 EMERGENT-K (LEVELS A-C) 60
Guided Reading for Emergent Readers 60
Introducing Books 61
    Teaching Points and Strategies 62
Prompting Strategies 62
    Cross-Checking 63
    Reading the Book 63
Word Study Strategies 64
    Sight Words Review 64
    Introducing New Sight Words 65
    Word Solving Strategies 65
Guided Writing 66
Guided Reading 67
    How to structure your guided reading session 67
Literacy Stations 68
Guided Reading or Word Work Group? 70

CHAPTER 6 EARLY READER-GRADE 1 (LEVELS D-I) 71
Guided Reading for Early Readers 71
Introducing the Book 72
    Teaching Points and Strategies 72
    Prompting strategies 75
Ways To Make Connections 75
Guided Writing 76
Guided Reading 77
    How to structure your guided reading session 77
Literacy Stations 78

CHAPTER 7 TRANSITIONAL READER: GRADES 2-3 (LEVELS J-N) 81

Guided Reading for Transitional Readers 81
Teaching points and strategies 82
Prompting strategies 84

Discussing Text 84
Fiction 85
Nonfiction 88

Guided Reading 90
How to structure your guided reading session 90

Literacy Stations 91

CHAPTER 8 THE FLUENT READER: GRADES 4-8 (LEVELS O-Z) 95

Guided Reading for Fluent Readers 95
Teaching points, strategies, what to assess 96

Discussing Text 97

Prompting 97

Guided Reading 98
How to structure your guided reading session 98

Literacy Stations 99

CHAPTER 9 PROMPTING TIPS 102

Why Prompting Is Important 102
Monitoring 102
Decoding 103
Fluency 103
Vocabulary 104
Comprehension 104

CHAPTER 10 TIPS FOR INTRODUCING TEXT 106

Introducing the Book..106

Understand the Message and Characters...107

Consider Learning Opportunities...108

CHAPTER 11 GUIDED READING TIPS FOR PARENTS 110

Guided Reading at Home 110

Routines and Independence 111

Choosing Text...111

Quick guide for parents for level reading text:................................*112*

The Five-Finger Strategy *112*

Keep It Fun! 113

CONCLUSION..115

DOWNLOAD YOUR FREE GIFT BELOW:.................................116

CHECK OUT OUR OTHER *AMAZING* TITLES:.......................118

The founders of NLP...*120*

Disassociation...121

Benefits of Dissociation 122

Easy NLP Disassociation Technique...122

Plan, Execute, Assess, Repeat *133*

Planning Stage...*134*

Execution Stage...*134*

Evaluation Stage..*135*

Essential Principles of a Time Management System 135

It Must Be Simple..*135*

It Must Be Complete *136*

It Must Be Connected..*137*

It Must Be Realistic...*137*

Ways of Setting Priorities 137
ABC Analysis 137
Pareto Analysis 138
Eisenhower Method 140
REFERENCES 142

Go from Stress to Success with These 15 Powerful Tips

You're in The Tunnel, Now Turn on The Light:

Here are The Best Ways to Transform Your Success

Do You Feel Stressed-Out, Overwhelmed and Harassed Every Day?

Then you're stuck in a negative thought spiral that is keeping you from achieving *real success!*

How many times have you thought, 'if only I could be more productive, then I'd get ahead?' No matter how hard you try, it eludes you. Most people experience intense self-doubt, worry and negative thinking at some point in their careers. These are your immediate obstacles to success.

Dr. Herman Kynaston

This guide tackles these issues with easy, direct solutions to help you break the cycle and get back on track. These 15 powerful tips will take you from overwhelmed to overjoyed, in no time!

This FREE Cheat Sheet contains:

- Essential tips on how to stop worrying and start living
- How to actually relieve anxiety and banish it for good
- Ways to get rid of negative thoughts, and how to stop them from recurring
- Tips to become the most productive, motivated version of yourself
- How to focus on career success and build positive cycles and habits

Scroll down and click the link **below to Claim your Free Cheat Sheet!**

I want you to know that you don't have to live this way. You don't have to feel like these negative cycles are getting the better of you. Your career is waiting to bloom – and flourish! Give yourself the opportunity to make the right choices, by learning how to authentically reach for lasting success.

Ditch the stress, embrace success.

Click Here!

Book Description:

Be the teacher who inspires the students to read with confidence and spirit!

Do you often find yourself thinking about how best to inspire students to read books?

Are you worried about the next PA meeting where you'll have to explain to parents why their kid can't keep up with their classmates' reading abilities?

Alternatively, are you noticing that you're **losing the attention of the advanced readers while introducing a lighter material?**

It almost looks like there's no way out of this situation, and that maybe you'll have to sacrifice some kids' learning in order to help the others.

"What am I doing wrong?" You may ask yourself. *"Am I not doing enough?"*

And you spend yet another night looking for a way to encourage and inspire the kids to read independently, identify words, and level with their peers.

The truth is, some teachers don't even ask these questions and then judge their students as talented or not talented when the difference lies in their **individual skills and development.**

Dr. Herman Kynaston

Numerous studies show that the traditional method of memorizing words and phrases only works with kids who learn to speak and recognize situations. That being said, **the old ways of forcing a kid to "just read the book" are obsolete.**

In *The Super Reader Protocol: The Guided Reading & Reading Comprehension Blueprint*, you'll discover:

- What kids know about reading books that you don't (yes, sometimes the student can even become the teacher!)

- A step-by-step guide on how best to prepare you and your students for a reading session, minus the frustrations

- The 5 engaging activities every teacher should use to help their students understand and decipher difficult words

- The secret to being the most helpful learning resource to your students *without burning out on the job*

- The key tasks you should be focusing on that other teachers consider "a waste of time" (hint: they're wrong!)

- The 2 main components to guided reading that you need to implement into your teachings today to see a 70% increase in your students' interest

- The psychologist-recommended way to continue to see progress in the kids' reading skills when they're out of the classroom

And much more.

Everyone learns at various paces and in different ways--we all develop uniquely, which can sometimes pose as a challenge for teachers. But when you know this, you also know to **expand your resources** to cater to all scenarios.

Watching a child transform into a confident bookworm is a wonderful sight. It's worth spending the time and energy needed if it means finally seeing all your students find the joy in reading.

If you want to introduce a creative method to your teaching plan and encourage your students to read, then scroll up and click "Add to Cart" right now.

Introduction

The traditional way of teaching a child to read, write, and spell is simply to teach them how to memorize words or letters. While this may have helped children read in days past, it has often left many more lagging behind the rest of the class. This uncertainty in their own ability to properly read, spell, and write can often lead to a distaste for reading.

Reading is such a vital component to a child's success in the academic setting that much pressure is placed on them to learn at younger ages and to read what is assigned to them. Students are often asked for facts in the story, but rarely about the opinions that they may have around a text they read. How can a child or young adult learn to fully enjoy reading when all they are taught is that reading is not pleasurable?

Guided reading challenges the traditional ways of teaching. It offers students and teachers a highly effective approach to reading instruction that not only encourages reading for academic purposes but personal purposes, as well.

Guided reading uses a differentiated approach that allows teachers to better understand and encourage reading from students based on the child's individual needs. When a child struggles to read at the same level as her peers, she can often struggle in many areas of the academic setting. She will often lack the confidence to pursue challenging career options or think she will not be able to make her parents proud.

The Super Reader Protocol

With this method, teachers are able to take a struggling reader and lead them into reading with fluency. It can take a student who is uncertain of how to make sense of what he reads to a student who confidently reads out loud and finds meaning in the text. The goal of guided reading is to teach students to read independently. They do so by learning various strategies that best help them with what they are struggling with most at the time.

When guided reading teachers take the time to properly evaluate and identify the skills students already possess, they can use those skills to build a wide range of literacy strategies. These strategies can be used to help overcome any difficulties they face while reading and allow them to move on from learning to read to reading to learn.

Teachers can easily implement guided reading sessions into their lesson plans. This process will allow them to teach the whole class what is required of them while also putting a focus on helping each individual child strengthen her reading and comprehension skills. The skills students learn and develop will then carry over and be used throughout the entirety of their lives.

This book, though meant for teachers, can benefit teachers and parents alike. You will learn the whole process of how to prepare your classroom for guided reading and a wide range of activities that will promote and encourage students to utilize various strategies and techniques to amplify their reading knowledge. You will learn how to structure guided reading effectively for readers at all levels so that every student in your classroom benefits from the process. Parents will also learn how they can continue the same technique at home.

This book comes with FREE Bonus chapters as a gift. You can download them for free. The free content can be found at the bottom of this book.

Chapter 1
Guided Reading in the Classroom

"The more that you read, the more things you will know. The more that you learn, the more places you'll go."

- Dr. Suess

The Importance of Guided Reading

Guided reading aligns with a student's needs. This approach to teaching allows students to learn and advance their reading skills through a process that is designed especially to meet their level of understanding and comprehension.

As such, guided reading gives teachers the opportunity to observe a child's reading ability and adjust the level of learning to a child's strengths. Guided reading incorporates small group readings and prompting instructions that help a child better understand text and reading material. Guided reading paves the path for children to develop a lifelong love of reading. By learning how to comprehend what they read through engaging instructions, they are able to transfer these skills immediately and apply them to understand more complex texts.

This approach to reading exposes a child to various texts on a daily basis. It helps them build the confidence and skills necessary to become excellent readers. Because of the small group teaching arrangement, children learn to read at a rate that encourages and supports their needs. They are able to fully understand what they are reading in a setting structured around their level of literacy.

The guided reading process benefits children because it helps them think more clearly about what they read. Through group discussion and writing activities, students not only learn to love specific genres, but they also strengthen their writing skills as well. Guided reading sessions tend to dedicate time for each child to read the assigned text. Then, through teacher prompting, students are encouraged to think about specific aspects of what they read. The teacher observes and guides the lessons based on the strengths of the group. The students do the reading and the teacher provides feedback or assists in correcting mistakes as they occur.

Small group sessions meet the needs of all students so they all advance together. This synergy is vital to encourage an interest in reading and to develop a desire for further reading skills. How is this beneficial? The classroom is a mix of all reading levels. Most students become discouraged and may give up quickly because they are unable to keep up or meet the expectations placed on them. If this scenario is reversed and students at a higher level are expected to read at a lower level, they can quickly lose interest and desire to progress. Each scenario discourages some of the students while assisting others. Guided reading eliminates these issues by allowing all readers to advance in groups or with the assistance needed for them to be successful.

Encouraging Independence

The goal of guided reading is to encourage children to become independent readers. This means children can work through challenging texts or words to be proficient readers on their own. Through guided reading, teachers do just that—guide the students. While they prompt students to discuss their text, the main role for them is to observe and determine the best approach to help the child read with confidence and excitement.

Guided reading was developed to ensure that students stay on track with required reading levels implemented by school and state guidelines but also to motivate them to excel. Since reading is such an integral part of school, it is vital that students learn this crucial skill. The inability to read will affect them academically for years. They will be unable to complete math word problems, retain information about social studies, or learn how to follow steps for science projects.

Guided reading encourages independence using two key components. The first component is the small literacy session. These sessions establish a zone of acceptance and are judgment-free. Since many of the students in the group are reading at the same level, no child feels left out or left behind. Each child is given an equal opportunity to read and learn at a rate that is fit for their skill level. The second way to encourage independence is through literacy activities. These activities are used during the small group sessions and through free time. The activities are vital to encouraging children to progress in reading. They are engaging and make reading an enjoyable experience. Even if a student is significantly behind the reading levels of other students, these activities will allow the child to work through their struggles and think logically about the text they are presented with.

Independent literacy activities

Since group sessions tend to include only four to six students, other activities need to be available to the rest of the classroom so you can give the group your attention. This requires setting up expectations and having a routine in place that lets the other children in the class know what they can do while sessions are taking place. Instead of handout busywork or worksheets, you can help encourage independent reading with literacy stations.

Literacy stations address various aspects of the reading process like:

- Letter recognition
- Vocabulary
- Spelling
- Grammar (for older children)
- Plots
- Character development

These activities should cater to all reading levels. There are a variety of ways you can approach literacy stations. For younger children, you might need to designate each child to a specific group with instructions on what order they need to work through the stations. You can use a timer that will allow the children equal time at each station. Older children may benefit more from being able to decide which they want to work on for themselves.

It is crucial to take time to establish a routine that will allow group sessions to be conducted while the other students participate in independent activities. This is something you can practice for the first two or three weeks at the beginning of the school year.

Literacy station ideas:

- Letter-sound workstation
- Sound station
- Partner reading
- Spelling and vocabulary reading
- Writers center
- Independent reading

You can set up as many stations as you wish, and you don't need to use every station each time there is a small group work being conducted.

Guided Reading Process

The before, during, and after approach to guided reading allows the teacher to support students through an entire reading process tailored to the student's needs. It addresses how to introduce the text, how to encourage students to work through challenging texts, and gives students time to reflect on the material and take part in comprehension activities to help students look at reading from an independent perspective.

1. Before reading

Setting the stage before you introduce the text is a vital step for students to begin learning and gaining interest in the text. The before reading stage is where students will gain an understanding of vocabulary, reading strategy, and the background of the text. Students will learn why the text was chosen and what they can expect from the reading lesson.

2. During reading

The reading material is chosen based on the student's reading level. Each student in the small group setting is given the proper time to read the assigned material. The teacher steps in to help children work through difficult words and to ask questions to ensure students comprehend the text.

3. After reading

After reading the text, students are given the opportunity to reflect on the material. During this step in the guided reading process, the teacher utilizes prompts, activities, writing exercises and other tools to help students decipher the text on their own. These activities encourage students to think more intently about the material independently. Activities are a mix of gaining an understanding of the parts of the story, characters, setting, plot and other reading specifics that are both fact and opinion-based, and prompts that encourage students to think about the information in the text as they perceive it. You can also include other reading comprehension activities, like word study and sound recognition and relate it to the material they just read.

Additional Guided Reading Tips

Stock up on the necessary supplies. Things you will want to have ready for your guided reading sessions:

The Super Reader Protocol

- Leveled reading books (you will learn more about these in chapter 3)
- Binders
- Folders
- Pointing sticks, popsicle sticks, and/or bingo chips to help students follow along in the texts
- Dry-erase boards
- Dry erase markers
- Sticky notes
- Various charts to use for the breakdown of groups, scheduling of groups, strategies being worked on, and more
- Word wall
- Handheld printout of various literacy strategies
- Prompting question or cue lists

Chapter 2
Guided Reading

"Reading should not be presented to a child as a chore, a duty. It should be offered as a gift."

- Katie Dicammillo

Guided Reading Process

Guided reading is accomplished through three main steps: assess, decide, and guide. While each step may have specific steps or actions teachers should take, there is one key focus in each. Observe the students as they read to understand what they need. Thorough assessment is a key component to guided reading and regularly assessing students is necessary to ensure they are making progress.

Assess

When you begin guided reading in the classroom, you will first need to take the time to assess the child's level of reading literacy. Assessments and evaluation can be conducted by:

- Screening
- Monitoring
- Running records
- Diagnostic assessments

The Super Reader Protocol

Through these assessments, you will be able to determine the student's strengths and weaknesses. You want to focus these assessments on the following:

1. Reading habits and preferences

This component gives you insight into what your students are interested in reading or learning more about. By observing their reading habits and preferences, you can identify which students need more in-depth help and what thinking skills the whole class uses.

2. Developmental word knowledge

This assessment focuses on the student's understanding of phonics and phonological awareness. What you find from this assessment is how you need to cater to your word study instruction to meet the needs of the students. You can find activities that will allow children to broaden their understanding of vowels, constants, and letter groupings.

3. Comprehension with reading or listening situations

Like reading habits and word knowledge, this component of the assessment process allows you to identify the students' grasp on reading comprehension. This can be done as a whole class assessment where you can observe each student's ability to gain information and understanding of the material they are reading. From the information you gather through this assessment, you can adjust the reading material to strengthen the skills children need to develop in order to understand what they read.

4. Instructional level

The instruction level assessment is what will give you more clarity on how to guide each student using educational tools and activities. Not all children will do well with verbal directions; some may need visual, hands-on, or simplified instructions to develop their skills. This assessment will look at all areas of the reading process to determine how each student needs to be approached to encourage reading independence.

Each component of the assessment provides you with information to use the right skills and strategies needed to move the student to a proficient reader. These assessments can be done in a whole-class setting, while some can be expanded on through individual attention.

Decide

The 'decide' phase of guided reading is where you use all the information gathered from the assessment phase to create your lesson plans. Here you will decide on the best approach, tools, groups, activities and reading material you will use to help students reach their reading goals. There are typically four areas that need to be covered during the 'decide' phase.

1. Place students into need-based groups

You will begin to form your small groups after you have conducted two to four weeks of observations. These groups can be easily changed as you get to know your students better and see they may benefit from a different approach than what is being utilized in their current group. When you review the assessments, you can begin to group students into the right small groups. How you approach this depends on what you feel will best benefit each student. The goal is to place students in a group with peers where social encouragement will occur and will allow each student to build the confidence necessary to further develop their reading skills.

Groups should contain four to six students, and they can be all at the same reading level, or there can be a mix of reading levels. How you set up the groups will require you to look over specific assessments conducted on observing how the students respond to different teaching strategies. Some students tend to shy away from participation when they do not understand the information. Placing a student like this in a group with an advanced reader might not benefit them but instead, cause them to become more insecure about their abilities. You want to push your students to learn the skills they need and build confidence in the skills they possess.

When you establish groups, you want each student to feel comfortable enough to share and participate in the discussion. Keep in mind that a group session with each group will not be possible to do every single day. You will want to consider how many days a week you would like to meet with each group. A general rule of thumb for scheduling group sessions is that you want to meet with the lower-level readers more often than the higher level. This doesn't mean you never meet with them, but higher-level readers can often do more reading on their own, where low-level readers may still lack the skills to be able to accomplish independent reading.

Steps for creating small groups:

Step 1: To begin forming your groups, you will first want to place each student in their current reading level category. It is possible that students may fall in between levels, where they are advanced enough to move to the next level but still struggle with the basic ideas that need to be understood in the next level. You can place students in between groups as well.

Step 2: Based on where your students fall in their reading development, break them into groups of four or five. The goal is to have the least number of groups in total while also being able to keep down the number of students in each group.

Step 3: Establish a schedule for your groups. Once you have your groups created, you should decide how many groups you will meet with each day; often, this will be two or three groups a day. Then you will determine how many days a week you need to meet with each group. You will need to spend at least 20 minutes with each group. Three to five minutes of that time is set aside to do individual or one-on-one work with specific students. This one-on-one time does not always mean giving more time to those who are struggling. Keep in mind that students who fall at a much higher reading level than the rest of the group will need dedicated one-on-one time to have the opportunity to work on more advanced reading the rest of the students are not ready for. Remember, you want to encourage *all* students to push themselves forward with their reading literacy. If you neglect those in above-average reading levels, they can become disengaged and unmotivated.

Step 4: Once you have determined how many groups you will meet with per day and how often you want to meet with them, you can begin to fill these groups into your schedule. Be flexible with your scheduling. As you start working with your small groups, you might find some students from different groups struggle with understanding certain concepts, such as plot, characters, cause and effect, and so on. When this occurs, you want to be able to schedule in time to pull these students together and work with them specifically on what they are struggling with.

You can set up a flexible schedule to allow for attention to be given to these special needs cases. A flexible schedule is simply your original schedule but with flexible slots established. These flexible spots will allow you the freedom to work with struggling or advanced readers to go over areas that are a struggle or to present new strategies to the reader that the rest of the class is not ready for.

2. Instructional focus

Now that you have your groups and schedule set up, it is time to decide what you will focus on during each small group slot. This will change frequently as your students begin to acquire the necessary skills that will allow for more complex material and concepts to be introduced.

The seven reading strategies of proficient readers:

- Activating
- Questioning
- Inferring
- Monitoring-clarifying
- Searching-selecting
- Summarizing

- Visual-organizing

Determine which strategy you want to focus on and incorporate into your group sessions. Each group will often have a different approach, as they will all be reading at different levels. Always keep track of what strategies you have worked on, how you worked on it, and when. You also want to take notes of how the students responded to learning the new strategy and tools used during the small group session. You need to avoid repeating what you have already done, especially if it was not very effective.

3. Decide on texts that will encourage thinking and problem-solving

The material you choose to use in your group session is crucial. If the material was too easy, your students will disengage and learn little. The text needs to allow the students to use the necessary problem-solving skills to increase fluency and comprehension. You don't want to be doing the reading *for* the students, so it needs to be at the right level. You also want to choose text that is of interest to the students. Through your assessments, you should have observed what types of genres or topics interest the students most. You'll want to choose the material with these preferences in mind.

Tips for choosing the right text:

- Choose text with familiar concepts.
- Choose engaging texts that spark the students' curiosity.
- Consider the elements of the story. Is the plot something the students will understand and find intriguing? Does the setting

of the story play a role in how interesting it is or will the student be able to recognize what the setting is?

- Choose a text that will require students to use the skills they already possess while reading.

- Are there a mix of words the students will be able to read easily and words that encourage the student to use methods to figure out more challenging words?

- Choose the right length material so students will have enough time to read through fully and allow for discussion time.

- Consider the text layout. Will the students be able to read the words with ease (are the words and lines spaced out correctly)? If there are images or graphics, how do these play a role in the material (will students be able to use the images to further understanding of the material)?

- Choose material that allows students to use problem-solving techniques, search for information, and check the facts while reading.

4. Monitor progress

How will you keep track of the progress each student is making? Monitoring progress is vital to ensure each student is moving at an expected pace that keeps them engaged and confident in the work they are doing. Tracking sheets can easily allow you to keep all the information needed so that you can look back and determine if you need to think about a new approach to help your students even further. Monitoring also informs you of what areas students are struggling with or how they can be given more challenging material to advance further.

Guide

The guiding process utilizes assessments to help teachers strengthen the skills students need to become fluent readers. Each student will have their own set of needs and goals to reach, but often you have a number of students who need to work on the same literacy skills. Through guiding and prompting, you will able to identify what their needs are and how to best encourage them to use strategies and techniques to enhance the comprehension of any given material. Through the guiding process, you will track progress and strategies used for each student and re-evaluate frequently to further help struggling students.

Use assessments to plan and teach

Guided reading is unique in the way it helps students use the skills and tools they already have to sound out words and understand the material. It is not the teacher who is simply reading the text to the students. Students are given an appropriate amount of time to work through a chosen text. The teacher provides prompts or reminders to struggling students.

Teachers guide students to think independently about the material. The teacher subtly reminds students of certain reading strategies that can help them through the text. The teachers' focus is on observing and providing support when necessary. Teachers will continue to assess students throughout the year and utilize these assessments to create a small group session around the reading strategies the students are struggling with.

Running records

Running records are one of the most effective ways to do continuous assessment both at a specific point in the year or as reading is taking place. Running records will provide you with the information you need to make your guided reading session plan the most effective. They can be used to:

- Choose the right text
- Chart student growth
- Keep track of strategies used
- Regroup when needed

Running records provide teachers with valuable information about a student's ability and thinking process. These do not just give you a place to mark how many words the child read wrong; it provides you with the knowledge of what the child already understands, what they are ready to begin learning, and what they will be able to work through and learn over the year. These records can pinpoint behaviors in the student that are holding them back from becoming excellent readers.

Running records should be conducted at the start of the school year to provide you with a baseline of the student's ability. They should be repeatedly done to measure progress and to determine what strategies need to be worked on more thoroughly. Running records will help you analyze:

- When children read a word correctly.
- They change a word in the text (counted as an error).

- When they have left out a word in the text (counted as an error).

- When they have added additional words to a text (counted as an error).

- When they have made an attempt to sound out a challenging word (counted as an error).

- When they had to repeat a line or word.

- When they had to ask for help during the reading (counted as an error, if the child is unable to read the word even with assistance, then it is counted as a word given).

- When they had to be told what a word was in the text (counted as an error).

- When they were able to self-correct during the reading.

To calculate the running error score:

1. You will need to have a total of all the words given to the child to read in the text.

2. Add up all the errors (see list above to determine what is considered an error)

3. Any full line of text that is skipped equals one error for each of the words skipped.

4. If an entire page is skipped, it is counted as one error, but you will count the total number of words from that page and subtract it from the total word count.

5. If a proper noun is misread multiple times, it only counts as one error.

6. Add up the total number of errors.

7. Subtract the total number of errors from the running word text. Then divide your answer by the total running words and multiply by 100 to get the accuracy percentage.

Calculate the self-correction rate:

You also want to figure out how often the child is self-correcting. This will give you a deeper understanding of whether the child is attempting to self-correct, may need to develop self-correcting strategies, or is already able to perform this task. To calculate the self-correction rate:

1. Add the total number of errors to the number of times there was an attempt to self-correct.

2. Divide this number by the number of self-corrections.

3. The number you get will show you the rate of how many times a child attempted to self-correct per number of errors.

Once you have calculated the running score and the self-correction rate, you can use this information to determine if the text was the right fit for the student. If they had a percentage of 96% or above, the text was too easy and they should be moved to a higher level book. If the percentage falls between 93-95%, then the book is comfortable for them. If the percentage is between 90-92%, the text was a challenge and the child would need extra support if staying at this level. If the percentage falls below 90%, the text is too difficult and the student should be reading at a lower level,

Running records can also help the teachers learn the reading behavior of each student. These records focus on establishing the child's understanding of:

- Meaning cues, or if the child is able to understand the basic meaning from the text they are reading

- Structural cues, which refer to the reader's ability to recall their own knowledge of grammar and structure to check whether what they are reading makes sense or not

- Visual cues, focusing on the reader's ability to determine whether a word looks right

This information will reveal how much of the information that a student reads is actually comprehended. It also indicates whether the child is able to use strategies to self-correct when a word doesn't make sense, fit, or look right in the sentence.

Running record process:

Running records should be recorded so teachers can review and revisit what the student has read. The process is fairly straightforward and is accomplished in five steps.

1. Select a text that will require the child to implement a number of strategies to read through the text. The child should possess many of the strategies the text will require of them.

2. Intro the text to the child. Give background information that the child may need to know to understand the text. Then allow the child to review the text briefly.

The Super Reader Protocol

3. Begin recording and prompt the student to begin reading the text out loud. If the text is short, allow the child to read through the whole piece. If it is longer, allow them to read at least 150 words.

4. When the child is done reading, ask him to give a brief summary or retelling of what he just read. Asking him to retell the story will show you if the child:

    - Has a basic understanding of the material
    - Is able to tell about the actual events in the story
    - Properly sequences the events
    - Makes personal connections
    - Uses words or phrases from what he reads
    - Gives details about the characters and the setting or provides supporting details.

1. After the retelling, you want to know how much the child was interested in what he read. You need to note whether he enjoyed it or not, as choosing the right text during a guided reading session should take into consideration the interest of the students.

Once you have finished all the steps, you can then analyze all the information you gathered. Properly organize all notes on the student's strengths, skill level, likes, and other important information so you can look at this information when you begin your small group session.

Dr. Herman Kynaston

Zone of Proximal Development

The zone of proximal development takes a three-step approach to understand what skills a child already possesses, needs help developing, and will need to work towards acquiring. This approach helps teachers know where each child is starting and what they will need to improve upon with little guidance. By understanding these two factors, you can create realistic goals for each child to pursue.

This approach can help you give your students the additional encouragement needed to build confidence in them as they master their literacy skills. This can also aid in deciding how to set up your small groups. Though it is beneficial to have your session set up to address the needs of one specific level of readers, with the zone of proximal development, you might consider having a slight mix of readers in your group setting. Having a skilled reader can add support and a deeper understanding for those still working to master certain reading concepts.

The idea behind this is to provide the right amount of assistance based on the child's response to the guidance being given. Some children will need specific instructions given each time. Other students may need specific instruction and then these can taper off to less specific instruction or guidance.

Guidance can be given in three ways:

1. Through general encouragement, or by allowing the child to do what he thinks needs to be done without being provided with step-by-step directions.

2. Giving specific instructions allows the child to know what steps need to be taken.

3. A direct demonstration is done when the child needs to be shown or assisted through every step of the process.

Reading, word study, writing

Each guided reading session will help students develop skills through the use of reading, word study, and writing activities and prompts. Sessions will often cover the following key topics:

- Introduce text, which is done by the teacher and offers brief moments for student engagement

- Learning targets, as the teacher will point out specific parts of the text to prompt students to use strategies or think about the text to obtain deeper understanding of the material.

- Support and teach strategies. Teachers prompt students to rethink what they have read to encourage self-directed strategies. The teacher reviews specific strategies the group is struggling with prior to reading the chosen text for that day.

- Reading and writing connection. After reading the text, the teacher allows time for students to write and share their understanding with the group.

- Engage. The teacher poses questions that can get students discussing the text and sharing the understanding or point of view about the material. The teacher should also pose questions that help the students make connections with the text. The teacher should provide positive feedback on efforts made.

Tools To Help With Monitoring and Assessing Students

There are plenty of resources available that can make assessing, monitoring, and tracking the progress of students a breeze. Some apps can help you determine which books to choose for your small group session. Some of these resources and tool include:

- BAS Reading Record iPad apps
- Online data management systems (ODMS)
- Benchmark Assessment Systems
- Reading A-Z
- GRo
- Book Wizard mobile

Sample Observation Sheet

Student Name	Date	Group and Reading Level	Strategy Being Worked On	Observation

In the strategy column, you can list all the strategies being worked on as a whole group as well as techniques that each individual student is working on. You can also have a 1 to 5 rating scale that will allow you to quickly see how they are progressing with each of the strategies.

In the observation column, you want to take note of how frequently the student implemented the strategy being taught. You also need to make notes of additional reading issues that the students might be struggling with that would hinder their ability to use the strategy being worked on currently. For instance, you are working on getting the student to use the picture that accompanies the text to find meaning for what a word might be. You notice, however, the student seems to be looking too much at the picture and not focusing on what they are reading. This could be an indication that you need to utilize more text following strategies or cover the picture up until the text has been read.

Another example would be you notice the student is not using self-correcting strategies when they say a word wrong. This can indicate that they need to review sound recognition or phonic work.

How To Keep Your Groups and Students Organized

When you implement guided reading into the classroom, you will find that you will have a lot more additional paperwork and data to keep track of. Few teachers are enthusiastic about having to keep track of extra paperwork, so keeping your groups and students properly organized will reduce the clutter and confusion. As you become more comfortable with the guided reading approach, you might find and utilize your own system for organizing and keeping track of student progress. When starting out, utilize some of these simple ways to keep your guided reading plans in check.

1. Use binders.

You want to have a binder dedicated to each student, as well as for each group. The student's binder you may not have to access regularly—possibly just to update progress once a month or every other month. The group binders you will want to update at least once a week. Group binders will be where you keep track of all you have done and the goals you have established for students. It is where you can keep track of each student's progress, what material or text has been read, activities used in and out of group sessions, and any additional notes on the students in that group.

2. Color code your groups.

Using colors not only will help you easily set up schedules and find the right binders and activities, but it also helps the students as well.

3. Review your observations.

Look over information at least once a week from group sessions. This will obviously allow you to stay informed about the progress the students are making and certain activities or strategies you want to focus on in the future with your groups.

4. Be flexible.

As you observe your students, you will identify more pressing concerns that need to be worked on. While you want to have a lesson plan in place for your small group sessions, you also want to be open to changes when necessary. If you see the group is progressing with decoding strategies but notice they are struggling significantly with retaining information from the text, then you want to move from word study to comprehension. This is when having your activities organized and nearby will come in handy. Also, know when to pull someone to work one-on-one for a few minutes during or after your group session. This is when having flex time at your disposal will be useful.

Chapter 3
Guided Reading Levels

"The unread story is not a story; it is little black marks on wood pulp. The reader, reading it, makes it live: a living thing, a story."

- Ursula K. Le Guin

What the Reading Levels Mean

There are a number of systems that rate reading material and each is used to determine a book's level of difficulty. With the guided reading method, books are rated in alphabetical order from A to Z, easiest to hardest.

Reading levels help students, teachers, and parents find the perfect text. This way, students can build their skills at the precise level of their development. This system classifies reading materials based on the characteristics of the text. These characteristics can include:

- Word choice
- Vocabulary
- Length of book
- Length of sentence
- Sentence complexity
- Subject matter

- Repetition and patterns
- Predictability
- Pictures, images, and/or illustrations
- Interest level
- Appropriateness of subject matter

Each level of books provides variation in aspects of the book and how they may be difficult for the reader, such as language, sentence length, vocabulary or reading concepts. Books are chosen based on the student's level of:

- Word knowledge
- Comprehension
- Fluency (accuracy, expression, phrasing, and speed)

Overview of Reading Levels

Reading levels are not necessarily based on grade level, though students in specific grades tend to fall into a limited range of reading levels such as:

- Kindergarten = Levels A-D
- 1st grade = A - I
- 2nd grade = E - N
- 3rd grade = J - Q
- 4th grade = M - T

- 5th grade = Q - W
- 6th grade and beyond = T - Z

Levels can, and often do, overlap from one grade level to the next. When you are creating your groups, you will first identify which levels your students fall into. To give you a better understanding of the types of books that fall into each of these levels, review the following list.

Level A - These books tend to have only one sentence or line of text per page. They utilize word patterns and sight words in connection with corresponding images. The fonts are large for easier reading and they are short, with the average being around eight pages long.

Level B - Level B books are similar to Level A books. They continue to use patterns, simple sight words and pictures to help tell the story. The main difference between Level A and Level B books is that B-level books contain two sentences or lines per page.

Level C - Level C continues to build upon the foundation students have gained from the Levels A and B books. Level C books will run slightly longer and include decodable words and words containing one or two syllables. They still use images along with text, and there are between two and five lines of text per page.

Level D - Level D books get into more complex stories. While similar to Level C books, these books lengthen their lines of texts. Pages may contain five lines and will have six or more words per sentence.

Level E - Level E books start to wean out pattern sentences. The stories are more complex and are longer than those in previous levels. Each page will have between two to eight lines of text and sentences will begin to run from one line and into the next.

The Super Reader Protocol

Level F - Level F books present stories that have a clear structure with a beginning, middle, and end. The fonts begin to get smaller as sentences now contain 10 or more words.

Level G - Level G books follow the form of Level F books. These books begin to incorporate three-syllable words and introduce more complex story ideas. They tend to challenge students with a wider range of vocabulary as well.

Level H - These books contain words that are composed of two or more syllables. The font decreases slightly more than that used in Levels F or G books. This level reduces repetition and introduces more vocabulary and challenging ideas.

Level I - Level I books begin to introduce various themes in the stories. Sentence structure adds in a mix of complex and compound sentences.

Level J - Level J stories will see a reduction in images with the text. Some books may break the story up into chapters. The text on each page can run from three sentences and up to twelve lines. The student will be introduced to more challenging spelling patterns.

Level K - Level K books follow the same layout as Level J books. These books, however, will be longer.

Level L - Level L books help students transition from the illustrated books they have used in the previous levels. The layout of these books shifts to include more chapters. These books often have 60 to 100 pages with little to no images accompanying the text. There can be five to 24 lines of text that will include four-syllable words.

Level M - Level M books introduce more complex plots with multiple characters to tell the story. They will often have no illustrations and the stories will be longer.

Level N - Level N books continue to build on the form of Level M books while presenting students with more challenging concepts.

Level O - These books are very similar to Level N but continue to challenge students through characters, themes, plots, and vocabulary.

Level P - Level P books introduce the use of figurative language more often. They tend to have more complex themes than level O, N, and M books.

Levels Q to W - This range of levels tends to build upon the skills students already know. By this time, students should be able to read independently and know what skills to access in working through challenging vocabulary and deepening their understanding of the texts. Books will begin to lengthen and may also include book series, which require readers to retain information from one book to the next. They will also introduce different styles of dialogues and plots, combine themes, and include various character types.

Levels X, Y, Z - These final levels introduce more complex storytelling techniques, such as storytelling through flashbacks, memories, or montages. More challenging vocabulary and more mature themes and storylines are common.

Leveled Literacy Intervention

While guided reading helps students learn the complexity of reading at their own rate and based on the skills they already have, some students may be a great deal further behind and struggle significantly more than others. In these cases, an intervention may be necessary to bring these students up to the same level of their peers. Leveled literacy intervention is a short-term process that streamlines the students reading and writing capabilities through more advanced strategies.

Leveled literacy intervention is for those students who are not meeting the grade level expectation. These intense small group session focus on:

- Close reading to expand the student's comprehension level
- Multiple texts and materials for the student to read daily
- Engaging the student(s) to build their literacy knowledge
- Monitoring the progress of the struggling student closely

These interventions are short-term and paced so students can quickly learn the necessary skills to join small session groups where they will be able to deploy their new skills immediately. These sessions should boost students who are struggling and lagging behind the rest of the class, so they are brought up to speed and can participate confidently alongside their peers. This is beneficial for students where English is a second language and provides support for children to quickly learn the fundamentals necessary to do well in the classroom. This is also beneficial for those students who do not meet their grade level expectancy and therefore are unable to participate and learn through the instruction given in the classroom.

Guided Reading Categories

Each reading level can be further organized into specific categories. These categories help determine the further complexities of the reading material according to benchmarks each book will contain across all levels. These categories, or benchmarks, include:

1. Genre

Genre refers to the type of book. The most common genres used in guided reading include:

- Realistic fiction: Made-up stories that could take place in real life and use familiar places as a setting

- Historical fiction: Stories that did not happen but are based on actual events; they tend to take place in the past and are adventurous

- Science fiction: These are made-up stories that tend to take place in the future and have some type of connection with technology or science topics.

- Fantasy: These stories are completely made-up and have elements in the story that are magical or supernatural; most of the concepts or situations in these stories could not occur in real life, such as talking animals or alternate worlds.

- Mystery: Mystery books tend to include most crime stories or stories where a mystery needs to be solved or something hidden is uncovered; these stories offer lots of little important details that require readers to follow closely.

- Biographies: These are texts that are written about someone's life based on someone else's view.

- Autobiographies: Autobiographies are texts that are written about a person's life and are actually written by the person.

- Traditional literature: This genre includes folk tales, fairy tales, or other stories that have been passed down from generation to generation.

- Poetry: Specific text that utilizes rhyming and sentence structure

- Fiction: Books or stories that are based on events that did not actually occur.

- Nonfiction or informational material: This genre covers material where factual information is provided on a wide number of topics like animals or historical events.

2. Text Structure

The structure refers to how the book is organized and presented to the reader in order to clearly reveal ideas or concepts in the text.

3. Content

Content is simply what the material is about. This basically summarizes or gives details about what type of information can be found or expected when reading the book.

4. Themes or ideas

The theme and ideas are the underlying purpose of the book. These are not always obvious and as students progress through the leveled reading books, themes and ideas become much more complex.

5. Language and features

This has to do with how the writer has written the book. It is wise to understand what new language or features a book may contain that can confuse readers if they haven't been exposed to this style of writing yet. These are things you want to consider pointing out when you introduce a new book to your guided reading session.

6. Sentence structure

This identifies how complex the sentence structure is throughout the book.

7. Vocabulary

Vocabulary identifies how many new words can be expected when reading this book.

8. Words

The words refer to how easily the words used in the text can be decoded and understood by the reader. This will relate to the reader's understanding of how to use decoding strategies to figure out how to read new words.

9. Illustrations or images

How many pictures or images are used throughout the book? Illustrations also take into account how well the exact text on that page can connect with the illustration or graphs shown.

10. Book layout

Book layout covers print size, lines per pages, illustrations and anything else that has to do with how the book is presented for readers. Book layout should be considered when readers are just getting into reading. Larger text and illustrations can help readers better use strategies to comprehend what they read and to utilize self-correction tools.

Getting Started Tips

1. Prepare the classroom.

Have your library of books already sorted by reading levels. This will make it easier for students to find the right books based on their reading abilities. Have a dedicated teaching table. You want your small group work to be done in a location that will get less traffic from other students and will have minimal distractions. You also want this teaching table to be set up in a way that encourages group discussion. Keep desks grouped together or get a kidney-shaped desk that helps everyone see each other. You want to provide a teaching setup that allows for easy observation and quick access to guidance.

2. Stay organized.

Organize the teaching table and area with all the resources you will need close by. You want to have all your material ready to grab and use when it comes time for a group session. You also want to keep all your activities and tools properly organized in case you need to make a slight detour from your intended instruction to go over something that would better benefit the group.

Keep your activities organized by strategy, such as word recognition, decoding, story structure, character developments, phonics and so on. This will help you go directly to the strategy to find the activity you need. Keep all groups organized in binders and have lesson plans and focus points already scheduled into the lesson. It can take time to get into a smooth routine with your guided reading groups, and when you first begin guided reading lessons, it will be a great deal of trial and error. As you continue to practice the steps, you will find a flawless system that works for you.

3. Have a clear routine.

Set up routines that encourage independence. They are not just viable to let children know what to expect during the session and to provide structure, but you also want this routine to provide them the opportunity to work on their skills on their own. Ensure that students understand that when you are working with a small group, they will need to work independently. This can be challenging with younger children, but the standards and expectations of the classroom can be established early on. When you set up your teaching table, consider how the other students in the classroom can have a visual cue and reminder for them not to disturb you or the other children in the small group. An obvious exception for interruptions is acceptable such as an injury, illness or other incidents that need to be addressed immediately.

4. Literacy stations.

Literacy stations are additional activities students can work through to increase their reading levels. While these are not required for guided reading, they are incredibly helpful and further encourage independent reading and learning. Literacy stations should consist of a variety of reading-based work, done through writing, reading samples, educational play, teamwork, and critical thinking. Each station should have varying levels of the same activities, so every student will benefit from participating. Set up literacy stations for the other students to explore while working with small groups. At the end of the following chapters, you will find ideas and suggestions for literacy stations that you can gain inspiration from.

5. Know what you need to assess.

Guided reading with small groups allow you to observe students as they read. In the process, you should be watching for how they are developing their literacy skills. You also want to be sure to focus on each student individually, so you know what will help him/her excel. Have a system that allows you to set time aside to evaluate the students' progress at least three times throughout the school year, as well as a way to make quick notes about lesson observations.

Chapter 4
Pre-K (Level Pre-A)

"Think before you speak. Read before you think."

- Frank Lebowitz

Guided Reading for Non-readers

At the pre-K level, you will mostly be working with non-readers. Children at this age have yet to learn letters or sound recognition. For most of these students, reading any Level A book is not possible. For readers, who are not yet at the A-Level, the focus is on developing the basics that will allow them to recognize letters and letter sounds, which will be the foundation of the skills needed to progress into reading.

Students should be assessed on the following criteria:

- Letter name knowledge

- Letter sound knowledge

- Name writing, able to say the letters in their name, and/or write their names

- Sound recognition or able to state the sounds they hear in a word

- Able to identify rhyming and non-rhyming words

- Handle books (knows how to hold a book properly, able to identify where the text is, may be able to point to letters or images)

Teaching points and strategies

- Identify the letters in the student's name

- Connect letters to their sounds

- Begin to write their name

- Able to match capital and lowercase letters together

- Identify letter shapes (curved, straight, hole)

- Clapping syllables

- Rhyming words

- Matching or able to identify words that begin with the same sounds

- Can state what the first sound in a word is

- Work on letter formation

- Understand the basic parts of the book (cover, title, author, illustrations, words)

- Understand print features (letters, words, sentences, ending punctuation)

- Space out words when writing

- Begin to write words according to sound

- Increase verbal vocabulary

- Can listen to a text and begin to comprehend what the story is

Letter Recognition Strategies

In order for students to begin reading, they must first have a grasp on letter recognition. At a young age, some students may be able to recite the letter in their name but may not be able to point out the letters when given the alphabet. The first step to develop literacy skills is to develop a child's letter recognition skills. Luckily, letter recognition activities can be combined with sound recognition and writing skill activities, so children are learning more than one element at a time. Below you will find some simple and effective ways to help students learn their letters and work through the ABCs.

Letter Sorting by Shape

This activity is helpful for those kiddos who have no grasp of letter recognition. This helps children learn to identify the shapes in each letter. For this activity, you can use letter magnets or letter cutouts. Have them learn to sort the letters by:

- Letters that have holes or no holes

- Letters that have curves or straight lines

More advanced strategies can include:

- Sorting letters that are the same into separate groups

- Sorting capital and lowercase alphabets; you can begin this activity by providing students with magnetic or foam letters that are two colors—one color for the uppercase letters and one color for the lowercase letters. As they are able to do this with ease, use one color for the lower and uppercase letters.

- Sorting the consonants from the vowels

Letter Hunt

Letter hunting is another ideal way for students to recognize letters. This can be done by dividing your students into four or more groups. Provide each group with a basket of ten letters of the alphabet; this can be done with letter magnets, cutouts, or foam letters. Then begin to call out random letters from the alphabet and have students find the letter, if they have it, from their basket of letters. Continue to call out letters until each group has found all the letters that were given in their basket.

Alphabet Book

Alphabet books are a great way for children to learn the letters of the alphabet. The covers of these mini-books display the letter students are working on. Inside the book are pictures that begin with the letter and space for children to practice tracing the letter.

The students can also create alphabet books. Provide each student with a blank sheet or two of paper. When you begin to work on a new letter, have them first write the letter in both lower and uppercase. And then have them draw and color a picture that starts with that letter. Keep all their pages in order and hold them in a binder for the children until the end of the year.

Letter Activities

There are countless ways you can have children practice and learn to identify their letters. Some of these activities can include:

1. Have children match lowercase letters to their correct capital letters. This can be done by having the capital letters printed on a piece of paper and then using magnetic or cutouts of the lowercase letters, which they would then place next to the right letter. If the kids have a solid grasp on their writing, you can have them write in the correct lowercase letters next to its capital.

2. Tracing letters is also a way students can easily learn the letters of the alphabet. This can also be done to identify the letters of their name. Simply have the alphabet and their names printed on a sheet of paper that allows them to trace the dots or dashes to complete the letters.

3. Provide the children with a sheet of paper that has a number of different letters mixed on it. Then have the children use a highlighter or simply circle specific letters on the page.

Sound Recognition Strategies

Once children begin to identify the letters, you want them to be able to match the correct sounds to these letters. Sound recognition activities can be highly enjoyable for children at a young age and there are plenty of games and puzzles you can expose children to that will make this process fun for them.

Picture Activities

1. Provide students with pictures of familiar items. Have students match the correct letter to the sound of the first letter they hear in a word. So if they are shown a picture of a hat, they would match this picture with the letter H.

2. Provide students with a sheet of paper that has a number of different images. Ask the students to circle or color the pictures that match the sound of a given letter.

3. Have students build mini puzzles of a picture that also spell out the word for the picture just below it. So they may have a picture of a cat, and the letters C-A-T would be below the picture. The puzzle only contains three pieces, so each letter stands on its own when the puzzle is not put together. These activities not only help students recognize the sounds of letters, but they also teach them a decoding strategy for when they are ready to begin reading.

Letter Hunt Using Words

This is similar to the letter hunt activity in the letter recognition category, but instead of calling out the letters and having the student find the right one, you instead say a word and the student will need to find the letter that matches the first letter of the word. For this activity, you will again divide your students into groups and provide them with a certain number of magnetic, foam, or cutout letters. Continue to say words until each group has cleared out all the letters from their basket.

Ways To Include Reading With Nonreaders

Though students at this age or grade are not ready to read text on their own, they can still begin to get used to reading by repeating lines back to the teacher and then reading them again on their own. Since many Level A books are concise and use simple words and have only a few words per page, this is great to help students gain the essential skill of reading.

Shared reading

Shared reading is done when the students and teachers read a text together. By doing shared reading, you can prompt younger students to use basic decoding strategies to read new words. This should be done with very easy text under the Level A category.

Echo reading

The teacher reads a line of text and the students repeat it back. Then students read the remaining text to themselves as the teacher provides help to students as needed.

Choral reading

With this reading lesson, the teacher and students will read an entire text together, with the teacher reading one line and the students repeating the line back. Once the whole text has been read, the students read the text again to themselves.

Read out loud

Readout loud is a way to help students develop their listening and comprehension skills. Choose a book at a slightly higher level then they would be able to read on their own. Then read the book to them as you ask questions about what is being read or to identify certain words or letter sounds from the text.

You can also use this to help children begin to identify rhyming words or to point out patterns or repetition in the text.

Letter Knowledge

One of the first skills children need to develop is the ability to recognize the different letters of the alphabet. Making this step in the learning process a game can help teach children to identify the letters instead of just memorizing the alphabet. The following activities can guide them to learn both capital and lowercase letters by engaging them to think about the shapes they see and the letters they may already recognize from their name.

Memory Game

This activity can be more challenging as it requires students to also remember the letters they see. Have a tray that displays three letters for the children to look at for a minute. Cover the tray and take one letter away, then uncover and see if the children can guess which letter was removed. You can do this activity with up to five letters on a tray or you can also just cover the tray and have the children recite what letters they saw back to you.

Word Building

Provide a word for the student with one of its letters missing. Ask them to fill in the spaces with as many letters as they can that will make an actual word, For instance, they can start with the word _ A T. They can fill the missing letter at the beginning of the word with a B for BAT, or C for CAT and so on.

You can do this with any of the letters at the beginning, middle or end of the word.

Introducing Sight Words or High-frequency

Words

Sight words or high-frequency words are usually the first words children learn to read, But this is often done through memorizing the word and not usually by reading the word. When introducing sight words, you want to also teach beginner decoding strategies that will help students learn how to break apart a word to read it. By doing this, you can begin exposing children to phonemic awareness too.

Word search

Have children find a new sight word in a mini-textbook and highlight or circle each word they find. Begin teaching students to use these words as anchors in the text.

Building words activities

- Have students build the sight word using magnetic letters or foam letters.

- Have students practice using the word in a sentence they create on their own.

- Have students say each sound of the letter in the word separately and then put all the sounds together.

- Have students add letters to sight words they are learning to create a new word. For instance, with THE, you can add an N at the end to create THEN.

Introducing Phonemic Awareness

When students begin reading, they need to have a good grasp on how the sounds in a word work together. The following activities can be used to increase a child's phonemic awareness and teach them strategies that will help them sound out new or unfamiliar words.

Using word families

Using word families in your teaching instruction will help young students identify patterns or features in certain words. They begin to understand that certain combinations will make the same sound, such as -at = BAT, CAT, HAT, THAT. Introducing the concept of word families can help students build up the vocabulary at a faster rate than simply introducing each word independently. Word families also strengthen a child's phonemic awareness and provide them with skills that will help them spell more challenging words later on.

Some examples of word families:

ACK = bACK, blACK, rACK, shACK, quACK

ELL = wELL, bELL, tELL, yELL, fELL

ALL = bALL, cALL, tALL, hALL, mALL

ASH = crASH, rASH, dASH, mASH, trASH, cASH, splASH

OP = hOP, cOP, tOP, mOP, flOP

UG = bUG, hUG, tUG, mUG, rUG, shrUG

You can begin introducing word families by using bookmark cards. At the top of the card, have a picture of an example of a word from that family along with what the word family is. Then list some of the words that fit into that word family.

Identify sound in words

Have children identify where they hear certain letter sounds. If you say the word did and asked them where they hear the sound "d-," they would respond with the beginning and the end of the word.

Things To Keep in Mind

You can begin to incorporate sentencing in with your plan for children who are more advanced. Have them cut out words to a sentence and arrange the words to create a complete sentence. This type of activity can help teach print concepts and left to right reading.

Some children have a difficult time with letter spacing and proper sizing when writing their names or letters. To help them get used to writing in a more consistent manner, you can use blocks for them to stay in when writing. For instance, children can practice this easily with their names. Instead of handing them a sheet of paper to write their name on the line, have blocks in place designated for each letter of their name. This helps them gain more control over their writing and focus to stay in the blocks when writing.

A Short message from the Author:

Hey, are you enjoying the book? I'd love to hear your thoughts!

Many readers do not know how hard reviews are to come by, and how much they help an author.

I would be incredibly grateful if you could take just 60 seconds to write a brief review on Amazon, even if it's just a few sentences!

\>> Click here to leave a quick review

https://www.amazon.com/review/create-review?asin=XXXXXXXXX

Thank you for taking the time to share your thoughts!

Your review will genuinely make a difference for me and help gain exposure for my work.

Chapter 5
Emergent-K (Levels A-C)

"I have a passion for teaching kids to become readers, to become comfortable with a book, not daunted. Books shouldn't be daunting, they should be funny, exciting and wonderful; and learning to be a reader gives a terrific advantage."

- Roald Dahl

Guided Reading for Emergent Readers

Students who are emergent readers have a clear understanding of letters and their sounds. They have a basic understanding of phonics and are able to rhyme or recognize patterns and syllables. At this stage, they will need to learn more about the complexities of constants and vowels (short vowels). They will be introduced to consonant-vowel-consonant (CVC) reading and more complex high-frequency words.

At this level, books should include:

- Pictures for support
- Controlled text
- Repetition in patterns
- Repeated vocabulary
- Large print

- Limited text per page
- Familiar concepts
- Wide spaces between letters
- Natural language

Children in kindergarten or early first grade will make up a majority of your students, though their level of reading can vary greatly. Some may still be working on sound recognition, while others are able to sound out words on their own. The strategies you use in the classroom will help them emerge from nonreaders to fluent readers, and from fluent readers to skilled readers.

Introducing Books

When introducing a book to such young readers, you will often need to be more straight to the point. You can begin by showing them the cover images and briefly explaining what the book is about. You want to avoid giving them the book when you are doing the introduction so as to maintain their attention.

Briefly go over concepts they might be unfamiliar with or ask questions that will help them relate to the text. For example, if you are reading a book that talks about siblings or family, then ask the students about their families. You can also give a little bit of background information about the book or author if it relates to the story. When you wrap up your introduction, you want to relate the information in the book to any recent experiences the students may have had or how they can use recent strategies to help them through the text.

Teaching Points and Strategies

With Levels A-C readers, teachers will often stick to expanding on these reading strategies:

- Learning to follow text from left to right; then being able to move on from simple left to right directionality and continue to follow left to right direction when there is more than one line of text on the page
- Matching words they hear spoken to words they see in the text
- Able to identify patterns in the text and are then able to notice how patterns in the text change
- Able to recognize words in a text and use these as anchors
- Able to identify the initial letter of words
- Can refer to the pictures to gain an understanding of what they are about to read or able to look at the pictures to figure out the meaning of the text or words
- Will reread areas or words they struggle with
- Can connect what they read to background information and can make personal connections with the text
- Begin to read more often

Prompting Strategies

Prompting strategies should help readers make sense of what they are reading and if what they read sounds right. This is a vital skill students need to develop in order to become independent readers. Prompting should focus on reminding students to use what they already know, what they can learn from the pictures that accompany the text, or what they sense from the text itself.

Prompting should encourage readers to identify when a word does not fit the text. It is not uncommon for many readers at this level to mix letters up, such as using B instead of D or M instead of N. When this occurs, you want the reader to be able to identify that the word they said does not sound right or does not make sense in the sentence. This will help them go back and try the word again. They can be prompted to look at the word again if they say the wrong letter, so they can try again and make the necessary corrections.

Cross-Checking

Cross-checking is a technique that will get students in the habit of identifying the first letter of a word with the actual word. With younger readers, this is done through a lot of pictures to test cross-checking, where the student will look at a picture and then find the word in the text. But this can also be done to help children identify new words they have not yet encountered. If a text has a new sight word that could cause difficulty, you want to find a page in the text that has this word and ask the students to point it out. This can be done when you introduce the book. And then you go back to the beginning of the story to read the whole thing.

Reading the Book

While reading the book, you want to have a few pages picked out where students can stop and go over what they have already read. Or you can ask students to use the picture to point out certain items and then find those words in the text. You want to encourage the student to talk about what they have read as it relates to the images on the page. Students who may be struggling more with reading may need to review the pictures first and then read the text. This can make it easier for them since the pictures help them form an expectation of what they will read.

Word Study Strategies

Students can learn a number of ways to read new words on their own once they have the basic foundation set. Some ways to teach students to decode words on their own:

- Have the student say the word slowly and identify what letters they hear. Then have them write the letters in the order they hear them.

- Have students clap how many syllables are in a word.

- Include common words that may be above their reading level, such as: because, said, are, were, there. These words are challenging to spell for new readers but can help them become fluent readers more quickly.

- Have students rhyme words and try to spell them out.

- Have students begin to identify different ways letters can come together to make the same sound, such as the "ou" in "out" and the "ow" in "down."

Sight Words Review

- Regularly review old and new sight words. This should be included at the beginning of your guided reading session. Have students begin to recognize word patterns or know which word families certain words fit into.

- Have children build words using simple sight words and see how many letters or different words they can create. Give them foam letters or magnetic letters to easily swap letters in and out.

- Have students identify the different sight words they see in a text by highlighting or circling the word.

- Picture sorting using medial vowels. Have students fill in the right vowel that will complete the word to match the picture.

Introducing New Sight Words

Have children identify words that look similar to the word introduced. Such as "at" in "that." This helps children begin to use what they already know to work through new words.

Word Solving Strategies

There are a number of ways young children can learn to work through words so that they make sense, sound right, and look right. This can be done by promoting the use of one of the following strategies:

1. The stretchy snake

With this strategy, the word should be stretched out, so each letter can be sounded out. Then add the sounds together.

2. The eagle eyes

Students can use the pictures to help find clues about what the word they are struggling with might be.

3. The chunky monkey

Identify a part of the word you do know. Remember word families, word parts, and strategies to build words.

4. The flippy dolphin

Try using a different vowel sound; instead of a short sound use a long, or vice versa, and see if the word makes sense.

5. The trying lion

Read the sentence again and use a word that might make sense in place of the word you are struggling with. What other words can you think of that have a similar reading to the one you used? Does the word you are struggling with look like it could be one of the similar words?

6. The skippy frog

Skip the word and finish reading the sentence. Go back and reread the sentence. Are there clues that can help you figure out what the skipped words is?

7. The lips fish

Say the first sound of the word you are struggling with out loud. Read the entire sentence, subbing in the first letter sound where the word is. When you are done reading the sentence, repeat the first letter sound. What do you think the word is?

Guided Writing

You want to continue to develop the students' writing skills. Exposure to reading words in a variety of ways can help them learn and begin to understand which methods help them learn better. Writing activities can be simple fill-in-the-blank exercises that will increase their fluency of reading simple words. Some writing ideas to consider:

- Have students fill in the missing letters of a word.

- Have students write words that rhyme with a given word.

- Introduce letter pairings: th, ch, sh, st, br, tr, and so on.

- Have students replace one letter of a word with another letter.

- Have students add on letters to a given word. For example, you can start with the sight word *is* then ask the student to add an *h* at the beginning and say the new word (his). Have the students add *t* at the beginning and say the new word (this).

Guided Reading

Here you will find a sample guided reading small group breakdown. It covers what you want to include in each session. You will need to keep track of who was in the group, date, what strategies you want to focus on, the book read, and key points from the book (you will list page numbers for reference) that will help students understand the material or use the strategies they are working on.

How to structure your guided reading session

Date:

Students in the group:

Teaching points/strategies:

Book being read:

Dr. Herman Kynaston

Key points:

(20-minute session)

- 3 minutes sight word review. Go over new sight words and decoding strategies to keep in mind while reading.

- 2 minutes book introduction. Go over the book you will be reading during that session, point out certain pages or words from the text and say why this text was chosen.

- 5 minutes of independent reading. Allow students to read the text on their own. During this time, you can observe and identify where students may be struggling while they read the text. Give prompts that will allow the students to work through challenging words and comprehend the material better.

- 5 minutes review. Retell the story and practice reading comprehension skills.

- 5 minutes writing exercise.

Literacy Stations

1. Independent reading. Students can choose a book that interests them and read quietly to themselves. Provide students with decoding strategies and thought-provoking instructions to keep in mind as they read. Have students spend a few minutes writing about what they read.

2. Partner reading. Have students read a text to one another.

3. Word work. Have activities that allow the students to practice spelling and phonemic awareness. This can include:

- Using foam letters to build a word
- Completing words by filling in the missing letters
- Identifying things in the classroom that start with certain letters or letter pairings
- Matching rhyming words
- Having students find rhyming words in a text or words that are in the same word family
- Word searches
- Rainbow coloring
- Using letter stamps to build words
- Using magnetic letters to build words
- Having students draw a picture to match words from a given list

4. Writing work

    - Have students practice writing new sight words or practice writing letters clearly.
    - Have different ways for students to practice writing, such as with crayons, using paint, or writing in sand with a straw.

Dr. Herman Kynaston

Guided Reading or Word Work Group?

Are your students ready for a guided reading group or should they be in a word workgroup? Before students can begin reading books with longer lines or sentences, they need to be able to use strategies that will help them work through new and challenging words. If students do not have a clear grasp on word work strategies, it can be more beneficial to group students into a word workgroup instead of a guided reading group. Word workgroups can be handled the same way as guided reading groups and are similar to what you have probably already been doing with the whole class. By implementing word workgroups, you can help students with the specific struggles they are having. Some students may be struggling to understand syllables while other students may struggle with letter groupings.

Before students can move on to reading sentence books, they need to have a grasp of word recognition and an understanding of the basic word parts. If you find students are still struggling with sight words or utilizing the word reading strategies, they might benefit more from a word workgroup to get them up to speed. They will need to have these skills when they transition into the early reader levels.

Chapter 6
Early Reader-Grade 1 (Levels D-I)

"Oh, magic hour, when a child first knows she can read printed words!"

- Betty Smith

Guided Reading for Early Readers

At the early reading level, students have a strong grasp of the alphabet and phonological awareness. They have a basic understanding of phonics and can identify a number of high-frequency words. Readers at this level can now begin strengthening their comprehension skills. They may have an understanding of fiction or nonfiction but can still expand on this knowledge to gain a better understanding of different reading purposes.

Early readers' books should include:

- One or more lines of text per page
- The introduction of complex sentences
- The opportunity for readers to gain a deeper understanding of topics
- Pictures that can provide a reference but are less important for understanding the text

Introducing the Book

Students reading at a level of F and above may not need a very lengthy introduction, but students still at D or E may need some more pre-reading prompting through the introduction. Typically, you want your book introduction to focus on the ideas or concepts in the book. At this level, students may be able to focus on reading with more accuracy but are not really retaining the information they read.

The book introduction at this level may vary greatly and you need to keep in mind the needs of the students. If the group struggles with phonics, your introduction should include a strategy or point out a section in the book that can strengthen their phonemic understanding. You may also decide to include an introduction with one or two new vocabulary words.

Your introduction should include what the book is about and what type of book it is (fiction or nonfiction) then ask a question that lets the students reveal their understanding of the subject matter. For instance, if the book is about the weather, you might ask them to name a few types of weather or ask what the weather is like that day. You can also ask them to describe different types of weather like hot for a sunny day. If there is a new word you know the students have never heard of before, you can ask them to turn to that page and point out the word.

Teaching Points and Strategies

- Able to spot high-frequency words and use them as anchors in the text and move on to being able to read these words naturally

The Super Reader Protocol

- Able to recall similar words to decode unfamiliar words (such as knowing the word "cat" and using that information to read the word "bat")

- Begin to blend the sounds within words

- Understand the end of word inflection: -ing, -ed, -s

- Reread challenging words or begins to self-correct words they say wrong

- Begin to use phrasing when reading

- Use their fingers less when reading text

- Begin to understand the use of punctuation

- Able to answer questions about the text

- Start to work on retelling the story

- Can make personal connections with the text

- Can make predictions of what the story is about based on the cover picture and title

- Make use of background information

- Can look through the word to read it correctly

- Begin to understand the different sounds of vowels and will begin to switch sounds if the word does not sound right

- Introduce phonics blending and use this knowledge through analogies

- Can begin to choose "just right" books based on their levels and skills
- Will make predictions about what will happen next in the book
- Learn to understand the difference between fiction and nonfiction
- Begin to understand the structure of simple stories, identifying the beginning, middle, and end
- Rely less on patterns within the text

Advanced strategies:

- Begin to use rhymes or chunks in words for decoding new words
- Understand what the table of contents is and learn how to use it in nonfiction reading
- Experience different genres
- Self-correct for accuracy and increased fluency
- Begin to use expression when reading because of an understanding of punctuation
- Able to revise a prediction made about the book as they read
- Can ask a question about the text that is appreciated for the level they read at
- Begin to understand the narrative structure and use this to retell the story

- Begin to make inferences or come up with a prediction or conclusion based on the information provided in the text without the authors coming right out and telling it

Prompting strategies

- Prompt to use self-correcting strategies.
- Use pictures to cross-check meaning in the text.
- Encourage the use of different vowel sounds.
- Increase their level of self-correcting by using problem-solving strategies.
- Read the book and retell it using beginning, middle, and end structure.
- Ask questions that help readers make a connection with the story.
- Ask students how they think a character feels at a specific point in the book. Why do they think that?
- Why do you think the character made a certain choice in the story?

Ways To Make Connections

Starting at a young level, students can begin to think more purposefully about what they are reading. There are many ways students can draw connections to their reading material. Some ideas that can encourage students to make connections include:

1. Personal experience. The student is able to relate to the text based on similar experiences they have had or something they have done.
2. Other books or reading material. Students can make connections to other books based on the types of characters, story, setting, or words used.
3. To something in the world. The material they read may make them think of a place or thing they know about.

Guided Writing

Guided writing approaches writing in the same manner that guided reading is done. This can be done in small group sessions or can address the whole class. Combining guided reading and guided writing allows students to gain a better understanding of the information they read and can support logical connections to the text. Some guided writing activities that can be done in small or large group sessions:

- Have students write about what they liked in the book.

- Have students describe a character from the book.

- Ask students to write about someone whom the characters from the book remind them of.

- Have students write a new word they saw in the text and draw a picture of it.

- Have students write words that rhyme in the texts.

- Have students write what they would do if they spent the day with one of the characters.

Guided Reading

Below is a sample of how you can run your small group session. Be sure to keep track of who was in the group, the strategies you want to work on with the group, the book and book level, and key points from the text you want to review before students begin reading.

How to structure your guided reading session

Date:

Students in the group:

Teaching points/strategies:

Book being read:

Level book:

Key points:

(20-minute session)

- 3 minutes sight word review. Go over new sight words and decoding strategies to keep in mind while reading.

- 2 minutes book introduction. Go over the book you will be reading during that session, point out certain pages or words from the text and say why this text was chosen.

- 5 minutes of independent reading. Allow students to read the text on their own. During this time, you can observe and identify where students may be struggling while they read the text. Give prompts that will allow the students to work through challenging words and comprehend the material better.

- 5 minutes review. Retell the story and practice reading comprehension skills.

- 5 minutes writing exercise.

Literacy Stations

1. Independent reading: Students can choose a book that interested them and read quietly to themselves. Provide students with decoding strategies and thought-provoking instructions to keep in mind as they read. Have students spend a few minutes writing about what they read.

2. Partner reading: Have students read text to one another.

3. Listen and/or recording: Students are able to listen to some of the reading material and then practice reading along with the audio version. Students can also record themselves reading to help them identify, in their own words, what they may have struggled with or words that do not fit into the sentence they read.

4. Word work: Have activities that allow students to practice spelling and phonemic awareness. This can include:

    - Using foam letters to build words
    - Completing words by filling in the missing letters
    - Organizing a list of words into groups by their phonic sounds
    - Matching rhyming words

- Having students find rhyming words in a text, words that are in the same word family, or words with the same phonic sounds

- Word searches

- Having students identify familiar words to practice decoding strategies

- Using letter stamps to build words

- Using magnetic letters to build words

- Having students draw a picture to match words from a given list

5. Sentence work:

    - Have students fill in the missing word of a sentence.

    - Have students unscramble words to make sentences.

    - Have students use the correct punctuation for sentences.

    - Have students edit a short text to find the mistakes.

    - Have students do sentence word search activities. Instead of a student looking for the letters to create a word, they have to find the right order of words that create a sentence. Then have them write the sentence.

    - Have students create their own sentences using specific words.

6. Writing work:

- Have students practice writing new sight words.

- Have students practice writing simple sentences.

- Have students keep a journal and write in it daily by choosing a journal prompt for the day. These journal prompts can vary in difficulty, such as:

    1. What is your favorite (food, color, class, etc.)?

    2. What made you smile today?

    3. What did you have for breakfast?

    4. Describe what you are wearing?

    5. What will you do after school today?

Chapter 7
Transitional Reader:
Grades 2-3 (Levels J-N)

"If you are going to get anywhere in life you have to read a lot of books."

- Roald Dahl

Guided Reading for Transitional Readers

Transitional readers are often able to comprehend simple reading material independently. Students tend to have an understanding of story structure and the basic story elements. Readers at this level should work on strengthening the skills needed to recognize and understand various types of genres. They should be encouraged to comprehend material independently.

Books for the transitional reader should include:

- Longer sentences, text per page, and stories
- Sentence structures or patterns that vary throughout the text
- Images and pictures that are not necessary for giving story cues
- A wider range of vocabulary
- Introduction of more descriptive language

Teaching points and strategies

- Able to use different strategies to decode new words
- Understand syllables, compound words, VCV patterns
- Can identify characters in different genres
- Introduced to series books
- Able to self-correct using the most appropriate strategies
- Will reread sections to improve fluency and accuracy
- Can read text with expression accurately
- Can use phrasing to read the text
- Able to gain the meaning of a word by looking for clues in the text
- Can retell the story using the narrative structure and language
- Will form opinions or begin to form their own thoughts based on the information provided in the text
- Will revise predictions while reading
- Can begin to identify characters written by specific authors
- Able to understand which strategies should be used when reading different genres
- Able to read silently
- Able to verbalize or write their understanding of text with more details

The Super Reader Protocol

- Able to follow the story through multiple chapters
- Able to read longer text
- Can begin to retell a story while injecting their own thoughts and connections to the material
- Understand what point of view is
- Identify character traits
- Begin to understand dialogue in text
- Consistently read books that fall into their "just right" or best-fit category, both fiction and nonfiction books

Advanced strategies:

- Begin to learn how to skim and scan material to find specific information
- Understand word parts (prefixes, suffixes and root word)
- Use word parts to decode new words
- Can begin to visualize what they read
- Can make inferences from multiple places in the text
- Can identify important events and facts in the text
- Understand of themes
- Understand character development, or how characters can change from the beginning to the end of the book

- Can begin to use nonfiction books for research

Prompting strategies

Prompting strategies should serve as a reminder that students have the skills to comprehend more challenging text.

Prompt students to look for the meaning of a word through information in the text. At the beginning of the guided reading session, remind students what they should take a quick note of while reading, such as:

- A question about a section of the text
- When they come across a new word
- When they thought something was interesting

Encourage students to visualize while reading. Visualizing allows students to create a mental picture of what they are reading, as though it were a movie be played to them. This process helps readers see what is happening and make connections based on the knowledge they already have. Visualization, while reading, also helps students think more creatively about what they read. You can help students strengthen this skill by choosing a place in the text that is descriptive or that can lead students to create a whole setting or picture around the text. When first introducing visualization, it can be helpful for students to actually draw out what they visualize. You can then ask them to share or explain why they created the scene as they did. You can then use this activity as a prompt to help students remember how to visualize while reading.

Discussing Text

The two main book types that students will be introduced to and continue to read are fiction and nonfiction. While each has subcategories, you want to get students to think clearly about the difference between the two types of genres and how they can enhance their understanding of what they read in each when presented with them.

Fiction

Fiction books will expose readers to a wide range of new elements to think about and gain information from. These elements include:

- Plot

The plot lets the reader know what is happening in the story. There are multiple plot points throughout the story that readers should learn to identify. These occur when there is a shift in the character or when a new problem arises that the character needs to make a choice on how to resolve the problem.

- Setting

The setting refers to where the story is taking place. Students can easily begin to understand setting by pointing out descriptive words about the environment, location or place, and time references.

- Characters

Characters are vital in fiction books and they can add a wide range of information the reader can think about to predict the outcome of the story. Most fiction books will have an antagonist and a protagonist. Some may have more than one of either. There are also supporting characters that can reveal background information that is vital for readers to know as the story progresses.

- Conflict

Conflict is a problem that needs to be resolved in the story. Different types of conflicts, including:

1. Character vs. character
2. Character vs. self
3. Character vs. environment
4. Character vs. society

- Theme

The theme is the message or lesson the author is trying to get the reader to understand. This is typically done through the characters as they try to resolve conflict and encounter other characters. Common topics for themes include:

1. Acceptance
2. Overcoming challenges
3. Courage
4. Teamwork
5. Friendship
6. Family
7. Love

8. Respect
- Main Idea

The main idea is what the book is about. This can usually be summed up in a few sentences. It uses supporting details in the text to back up the idea.

Prompting tips for fiction:

- Remind students to think about the setting and take note of clues that give information about the setting.
- Have them visualize the setting or draw a picture to recreate the setting.
- Have students identify what the plot is, where it peaks in the story and the resolution.
- What type of conflict is occurring in the story?
- Who are the characters and what are their traits?
- Who do you think is the antagonist or protagonist?
- What role does a specific character play in the story? Did they reveal information that might be necessary?
- How do you think the character felt at a certain point in the story?
- What did you learn as you read the text?
- What do you think the main idea of this chapter was? What supports this?

- How have the characters' opinions changed from the beginning to the end of the story?

- Think about a time when you had to face a challenge like one of the characters in the story.

Nonfiction

The text structure of a nonfiction book can be challenging for some readers to understand. There are ways you can help students understand the text structure of a nonfiction book—having them look for keywords that can give them clues, for instance. The types of text structure and prompts for engaging readers are:

1. Cause and effect

With cause and effect, nonfiction shares specific details on an event and the information needed to understand why the events occur.

Prompting tips:

- Ask the readers to pay attention to specific places, dates, and names provided.

- Have them look for words, such as if, when, so, cause, effect, and because.

2. Compare and contrast

With this structure, there are usually multiple ideas and topics discussed. The author points out the similarities and differences between these items.

Prompting tips:

- Have students take note of what seems to be described in greater detail.

- Have students take note of facts provided by the author.

- Have the readers look for words such as like, unlike, similar, both, different from.

3. Description

With descriptive nonfiction, the author is providing more in-depth information around a specific topic.

Prompting tips:

- Have students take note of descriptive words.

- Have students make a note of specific elements that relate to the topic.

- Remind students to look for words or phrases such as: for instance, to begin with, features, examples of.

4. Problem and solution

Problem nonfiction discusses a problem and may present a solution or possible solution to the problem.

Prompting tips:

- Have students identify what concerns the author presents.

- Have the students try to relate to the information provided in the text.

- Ask students to look for words or phrases such as problem, solution, since, the issue is, because, resolved by.

Guided Reading

Below is a sample of how you can run your small group session. At this level, you want to provide students with more reading time than you would with lower grades, as the texts are getting longer and more challenging. You still want to keep track of who is in the group, the strategies you want to work on with the group, the book and book level, and key points from the text you want to review before students begin reading. At the end of the reading portion, you should ask students questions about the text that will help them begin to think more logically about what they read, such as ways they can make a connection to the material or information they can gather from it. End each session with a writing exercise that relates to the material they just read.

How to structure your guided reading session

Date:

Students in the group:

Teaching points/strategies:

Book being read:

Level book:

Key points:

(20-minute session)

The Super Reader Protocol

- 3 minutes review of genre or character traits (should relate to the story about to be read).

- 2 minutes book introduction. Go over the book you will be reading during that session, point out certain pages or words from the text, and say why this text was chosen.

- 10 minutes of independent reading. Allow students to read the text on their own. During this time, you can observe and identify where students may be struggling while they read the text. Give prompts that will allow the students to work through challenging words and comprehend the material better.

- 3 minutes review. Retell the story and practice reading comprehension skills.

- 2 minutes writing exercise.

Literacy Stations

1. Independent reading: Students can choose a book that interests them and read quietly to themselves. Provide students with decoding strategies and thought-provoking instructions to keep in mind as they read. Have students spend a few minutes writing about what they read.

2. Reading comprehension and story structure:

    - Have students read a text and write about what happened at the beginning, middle, and end of the text.

    - Have students predict what the story might be about when given a sentence/title.

- Have students identify different characters from a provided text.

- Have students identify books as fiction or nonfiction based on a description of the book.

- Have students write out one interesting fact they found in a nonfiction book.

3. Word work: Have activities that allow students to practice spelling and phonemic awareness. This can include:

    - Completing words by filling in the missing letters

    - Word searches

    - Using long or short vowel sounds in words

    - Identifying nonsense words

    - Unscrambling words/How many words can they make with a certain set of letters?

    - Boggle/How many words can they find?

    - Matching words to their meaning

    - Having students read a text with a challenging or new word and see if they can find clues in the sentence that will provide them with what the word means; then, have them write their own sentence using that word.

    - Giving a list of synonyms or antonyms for a certain word

- Activities on word parts

4. Sentence work:

    - Have students fill in the missing word of a sentence.

    - Have students unscramble words to make sentences.

    - Have students edit a short text to find the mistakes.

    - Have students do sentence word search activities. Instead of students looking for the letters to create a word, they have to find the right order of words that create a sentence. Then have them write the sentence.

5. Writing work:

    - Have students practice writing new vocabulary words.

    - Have students practice writing simple sentences.

    - Have students keep a journal and write in it daily by choosing a journal prompt for the day. Journal prompts should encourage students to write two or more sentences in response, such as:

        1. What did you do over the weekend?

        2. What did you have for dinner last night? What would you have rather had?

        3. Write a letter to a character from your favorite TV show.

4. Write about something you love. Why do you like it so much?

5. Write about something new you learned today. How would you teach this to someone else?

6. Write about something you do really well.

Chapter 8
The Fluent Reader:
Grades 4-8 (Levels O-Z)

"If you don't like to read, you haven't found the right book."

- J.K. Rowling

Guided Reading for Fluent Readers

Students at the fluent reading level have a clear understanding of how to read. They are able to read longer lines of text and implement techniques that allow them to work through difficult words. At this level, students move from learning to read to reading to learn. Students will need to strengthen comprehension skills in order to pull information from the material they read.

Books at the fluent reading level can often be chosen by the reader individually. Students should be encouraged to read a wide range of materials to strengthen their comprehension skills. When performing guided reading sessions, books should focus on:

- Introducing a wide range of topics to the students
- Encouraging students to work through more challenging vocabulary
- Expanding the students' knowledge of writing styles
- Including more descriptive text with complex sentences

Teaching points, strategies, what to assess

- Use word parts to decode new words
- Can read longer books with multiple chapters
- Can easily make connections with what they are reading
- Can visualize what they are reading
- Skim or scan material to find specific information
- Can make inferences from multiple places in the text
- Can identify important events and facts in the text
- Understand themes
- Understand character development and how they can change from the beginning to the end of the book and why this occurs
- Have a clear understanding of different characters based on the genre they are reading
- Able to apply various strategies to gain a deeper comprehension of the material
- Clearly understand the point of view and can identify which point or whose point of view the story is being told from
- Define character traits
- Can understand text even when they have no direct connection or experience with the information they are reading
- Understand historical perspective

Discussing Text

When discussing the text, you want to focus on the student being able to properly retell or summarize the events that took place, in their own words but following the chronological order that appears in the text.

When the group has finished with the reading time, begin the discussion by first asking if there are any questions about any parts of the text. Also, ask what part of the text stuck out to them the most.

You can have students use prompting bookmarks if they struggle to take note of important events in the story. These bookmarks can have pictures or text that remind them to pay attention to character traits, plot twists, points of view and so on.

You can also provide students with a sheet that will allow them to answer the basic questions of story structure and features.

Have students go over the answers they provided on their promoting sheets and encourage others to elaborate or add to what the students say.

Prompting

- Encourage students to skim through the material and write what they think it is about.

- Have students skim the material to quickly answer questions about the material.

- Have students choose a character from the book and keep track of how the character's feelings change, things they did that had an impact on the story, or struggles they encounter.

- Remind students to visualize the information they read and think about what they would do in a similar situation.

Guided Reading

Below is a sample of how you can run your small group session with higher-level readers. At this point, you will be shifting your focus from word work and decoding to more complex ideas around the story and information. At the beginning of each session, you want to go over the key strategy the group will focus on, such as identifying characters, spotting genre trends, taking note of what happens at the beginning, middle or end of the story, and so on. These sessions will often have students read the same book across multiple days and will be provided with take-home prompts to answer or consider as they read parts of the book at home. At the beginning of each session, you will address the take-home prompts and ask students to share some of their responses. Then continue to read on with the book. At the end of the reading portion, you should ask students questions about the text that will help them begin to think more logically about what they read. For instance, how can they make a connection to the material, or what information can they gather from it? End each session with a writing exercise that relates to the material they just read or give them an activity they can work on at home.

How to structure your guided reading session

Date:

Students in the group:

Teaching points/strategies:

Book being read:

The Super Reader Protocol

Level book:

Key points:

(20-minute session)

- 3 minutes review of genre or character traits (should relate to the story about to be read)
- 2 minutes book introduction. Go over the book you will be reading during that session, point out certain pages or words from the text and say why this text was chosen.
- 10 minutes of independent reading. Allow students to read the text on their own. During this time, you can observe and identify where students may be struggling while they read the text. Give prompts that will allow the students to work through challenging words and comprehend the material better.
- 3 minutes review. Retell the story and practice reading comprehension skills.
- 2 minutes writing exercise.

You want to introduce students to a wide range of texts. Give students an opportunity to read some they choose on their own and discuss it during a group session. This can help the student develop their story retelling skills and can encourage others to discuss what else the book may be about. In a sense, you are allowing the student to be the teacher every once in a while. You can consider doing an activity like this once a month with all of the students.

Literacy Stations

At this level, literacy stations may take on a different look. Instead of having more activity-based stations, there will be more writing and comprehension exercises. Some ways you can approach literacy stations for higher-level readers include doing partner or group work or individual seatwork. Some ideas to spark inspiration include:

1. Partner reading.

Provide two different texts for each person to read. Once they have finished reading, each partner takes turns asking questions that will answer what the theme, plot, genre, characters, or information is about. The students should do this by asking a yes or no question but not direct questions such as "Was your text fiction?". (You can provide sample questions for students to ask.) Each student will write their own brief summary or prediction about what the other person's text was about. Then the students will give a overview of the text they read as the other person checks to see how accurate their prediction was.

2. Dialogue work.

This can be done with a partner or individually. Provide students with a dialogue excerpt from a book, and have the students read the dialogue together.

3. Skimming and scanning.

Provide students with a long list of questions based on a given text. Have the student skim and scan the text to try to answer as many questions as they can in a given amount of time.

4. Nonfiction to fiction.

Provide students with a short nonfiction text. Have them rewrite the text into a fictional story.

5. Writing prompts.

Students at this level should be encouraged to find deeper meaning in what they read. They should also be strengthening their understanding of the text and how they can come up with their own opinions or think more creatively about what they read. Some ways you can encourage students to think outside the box as they read is through various writing activities. Some writing prompts can include:

- Have them think about the choices the main character made in the story. Ask them to think about how the story would have ended differently if that main character had decided to do something differently. Have them write a different ending and explain why this would have occurred.

- Ask the students to think about how the story would be different if it took place in the present moment. How would technology play a role in the outcome of the story? Ask the students to come up with a new beginning, middle, and end to the story.

- For nonfiction books, ask the students how they can relate the information or problem they read about to modern times. Are there any problems with the world today that this information can impact?

- Have students identify the main theme of the story. Then ask them if they can spot any hidden themes in the text. Have them list what in the text supports this theme.

Chapter 9
Prompting Tips

"A children's story that can only be enjoyed by children is not a good children's story in the slightest."

- C.S. Lewis

Why Prompting Is Important

Prompting can be done before, during, or after the actual reading has occurred within your small group sessions. Promoting is done to not only encourage engagement but to help students know what to think about while they are reading the text. The right prompting can allow students to use the skills they already have and to develop stronger comprehension skills.

Prompting is also vital for teachers to continue to measure student progress and identify areas that students may be struggling to understand. Prompting can be successfully done by utilizing the following techniques and suggestions.

Monitoring

As a student reads and stumbles upon a word, you do not want to simply correct them and tell them the right word. Instead, you can use prompts to help them understand and make sense of what they are reading. You can do this by asking or encouraging the student:

The Super Reader Protocol

- Does that make sense?
- Check that again with your finger.
- Are you sure that is correct? Let's try that again.

Decoding

Decoding can be done by utilizing images that accompany the text or by helping the student break down the words. This can be done by:

- Referencing the picture and saying the first part of the word. Ask the student to look for what would sound right and make the most sense.
- Trying to break the word down into parts.
- What other words look similar to that word?

Fluency

Increasing a child's fluency will help them improve in various aspects of the reading process. You can help strengthen students' fluency by:

- Asking the student to read a line without using their finger to follow along.
- Asking the student to say a line the way a character in the book would say it.
- Asking them to read a line without putting as long a break or as many breaks in the text.

Record the student reading the text aloud, which will give you, the teacher, the ability to revisit the student's comprehension and fluency skills. Being able to re-listen to the students reading will better enable you to provide activities and prompts that will increase their literacy.

Some students may excel faster by first listening to the book then reading it on their own. Offer struggling students headsets so they can hear the story first, and then encourage them to read the story themselves out loud. Combine the reading out loud with recording them reading to help identify trouble areas.

Vocabulary

Expanding a child's vocabulary will help her feel more confident about reading challenging text. By encouraging students to use the techniques and skills they already possess to decipher and work through new words, you will allow them to use these techniques properly in the future. Some ways you can prompt a child to work through challenging vocabulary words:

- Ask if there are any words that the student does not understand in the text.

- Ask the student to look at pictures or words in the sentence that can help them understand what the word is.

- Ask them if they can identify a part of the word they do recognize. Then guide them to understand it as a whole.

Comprehension

Students can begin developing their comprehension skills even before they are reading. Comprehension focuses on understanding what is being said or occurring in the text. At a young age this is primarily done by using images to prompt students to come up with their own idea of what the story might be about. As students get older, it is the different elements of the story that will allow the student to fully understand what is going on. Ways you can prompt students to develop their comprehension skills:

- Ask students what is occurring based on the images on that page.

- Ask if there is anything that the students do not understand or if they are confused by what has occurred so far in the story.

- Ask the student to think about the characters in the story and why they do or say certain things.

- Ask them to find information in the text that supports the predictions they make.

- Ask them to make connections from their own perspective with the text.

Prompting for fluent readers may be more effective when given a question to think and write on. You can encourage students to think about character development by asking students to write what they think the character will do next in the story and why.

Chapter 10
Tips for Introducing Text

"To learn to read is to light a fire; every syllable that is spelled out is a spark."

- Victor Hugo

Introducing the Book

Creating a strong and enticing book introduction will capture the students' attention and make them eager to learn more. Since the introduction only takes a few minutes, you want to carefully craft these introductions specifically for each of your groups. The introduction isn't just about telling them what the story is about; it should also include strategies that will help strengthen their literacy skills.

Book introduction should set the stage for the readers. It should point out key details and encourage them to think logically about what they read.

When introducing the book, you want to:

1. Begin by asking about the picture on the cover or title of the book.

2. You want to keep the conversation casual and ask just a few questions for the students to respond to.

3. Go over ways students can help decode words or comprehend the text more thoroughly.

4. Bring up important ideas or concepts the students should keep in mind while reading the book.

5. Suggest a recent strategy the students have learned that will allow them to work through the text.

6. Let the student know why the book was chosen.

What you do not want to do when you introduce a book:

1. Go over every picture in the book and discuss what each picture might mean.

2. Not allow the students an opportunity to add their own ideas into the conversation. Or just talking to the students without asking questions.

3. Give away too many details of the story, especially the ending.

4. Expect students to make long predictions about the story or to guess what new vocabulary words mean prior to reading.

5. Go into a lesson about phonics, patterns, or comprehension strategies.

Understand the Message and Characters

No matter what level your students are at, one of the best ways to get them interested in reading a book is to offer them some interesting characters to learn about. Consider ways you can introduce interesting characters from the book and encourage them to make connections with this character.

- Ask if the character reminds them of a character from another book.

- Ask if they think the traits of the character might cause them problems.

- Ask them to identify their own traits in relation to the characters.

You can also hint about what the message of the book might be. The title and cover image easily give these details to readers, so be sure to ask what they think.

Consider Learning Opportunities

Based on their level of reading, what skills should the reader have or need to develop further? How can the book help encourage this growth? You want to ensure that the book you choose will help your students develop skills to become independent readers. When you are composing your book introduction, you should consider adding in one or two specific pages that the readers can review before reading to gain a deeper understanding of a new word, sense structure, or comprehension skills. Once you have identified these key areas and briefly reviewed them, go immediately into the student reading.

The goal of guided reading sessions is to move quickly through the talk about the text and right into the reading part. It is when the students are reading that you are gaining the most information on their skill sets and progress.

The Super Reader Protocol

Once students have begun reading, it is time to observe and take notes. Go around to each student one by one and provide them the right prompts, if necessary, to read through a challenging line. Once the reading has been completed, you can bring up some key points from your introduction and ask students to give their opinion about what they read in relation to what you mentioned at the beginning.

Chapter 11
Guided Reading Tips for Parents

"There are many little ways to enlarge your child's world. Love of books is the best of all."

-Jacqueline Kennedy Onassis

Guided Reading at Home

Teachers want students to continue to practice what they learn in the classroom outside of school as well. Inviting parents to take a role in the child's guided reading experience can further benefit the child and allow them to flourish as a skilled reader. When discussing with parents the guided reading process and focus, you want to ensure they understand how to implement the strategies at home.

Parents do not have to take assessments, but they should be able to guide their child's reading ability and play an active role in helping their child develop as a fluent reader. At home, parents should make reading a regular occurrence to encourage their children to read for pleasure and not just when they have to for school.

In this final chapter, we will discuss how parents can support their child's reading skills away from school. Teachers can use this information to provide parents with steps or suggestions to encourage reading at home.

Routines and Independence

Decide that you will take the time to read with your child. This can be done in a number of ways. You can help your child read through a book they choose, or you can read your own books at the same time with each other. Reading can be an excellent before-bed activity. The goal is to establish a routine that promotes the joy of reading. Encourage your child to read on his own, as well. Instead of watching television for an hour or playing video games, have your child read for half that time instead.

Reading books is not the only way you can help your child become a better reader. Just as in the classroom, there are a number of literacy stations and activities. You can come up with your own activities in the home to do along with your child. By encouraging your child to practice the strategies and techniques they learn in the classroom, you can help build their confidence in their abilities to comprehend more challenging text.

Choosing Text

You want your child to choose the books they read at home. Whether you visit a library, download a few ebooks, or visit the local book store, give your child the independence to choose the book that interests her. You can guide her toward the right level, so she chooses the best fit text.

Leveled books may seem intimidating, but this simple reference guide can help you determine which books your child should be looking at. You can gain a better understanding of these levels by revisiting Chapter 3 in this book.

Quick guide for parents for level reading text:

Kindergarten = Levels A, B, C, D

1st grade = A, B, C, D, E, F, G, H, I

2nd grade = E, F, G, H, I, J, K, L, M, N

3rd grade = J, K, L, M, N, O, P, Q

4th grade = M, N, O, P, Q, R, S, T

5th grade = Q, R, S, T, U, V, W

6th grade and beyond = T, U, V, W, X, Y, Z

The Five-Finger Strategy

As a parent, this wide range of levels can be confusing and overwhelming. Is your child ready for a Level I book, or would he benefit from reading a Level C or D book? Some parents may find that their first grader can actually complete a Level K or L book! One of the best ways to know if the book your child has chosen to read is appropriate for him is to utilize the five-finger strategy.

Have your child read a portion of the text as you keep track of how many words in the text they stumble on or are unable to read. If you have between less than two fingers up, the material is too easy for them. It is a good choice for them to read independently but not for the sake of improving their literacy skills. If you have over five fingers up, the book is too challenging and can discourage readers from wanting to continue reading. If you are holding up between two to five fingers, then you have found the best-fit text. This means there is enough new information in the material to encourage the reader to utilize literacy skills and read through the text.

Keep It Fun!

The last thing you want to do—accidentally or intentionally—is discourage your child from reading. This is why choosing the right text can be especially important. You want your child to have a good experience while she is reading. If you see her struggling, offer her guidance. Ask her what types of strategies she uses in school that she can teach you so you can help her work through the text together.

Be interested in what your kids are reading. Ask them questions about the story, characters, or events. This not only shows you want to help them, but it helps them develop necessary comprehension skills.

If you feel you may not be helping your child or you would like to know more specifics of how you can help your child enjoy reading more, don't be afraid to reach out to the reading teacher. Since the teacher has all the assessment information, notes, and observations, they can give you a better understanding of what your child is struggling with and some effective tips that can help you help your child.

The end... almost!

Reviews are not easy to come by.

As an independent author with a tiny marketing budget, I rely on readers, like you, to leave a short review on Amazon.

Even if it's just a sentence or two!

So if you enjoyed the book, please...

>> Click here to leave a brief review on Amazon.

https://www.amazon.com/review/create-review?asin=XXXXXXXXX

I am very appreciative for your review as it truly makes a difference.

Thank you from the bottom of my heart for purchasing this book and reading it to the end.

Conclusion

Guided reading is an effective way for children of all reading levels to develop and improve reading skills. Guided reading offers students a unique way to learn the various elements of learning to read and mastering reading through specifically chosen text and small group discussions. Through guidance, prompts, activities, and writing exercises, a child is able to find joy in reading from their earliest days.

Guided reading can be done at any grade level, though the earlier it is implemented, the more beneficial it can be for the child. Guided reading offers a different approach to reading for both teachers and students. It utilizes specific strategies that can help students learn to work independently through challenging words and deepen their understanding of what they read. Teachers no longer tell students what words are or wait for another student to answer questions about plot, theme, and point of view correctly. They guide students to figure out how to find the answer in the text themselves.

For so long, students have been taught to memorize sight words, spelling words, and story outlines that many never fully developed the necessary skills to decipher words, make connections, and learn to love reading. Guided reading gives students the tools needed to become masters of fluency and literature while encouraging them to constantly push themselves a little further outside their reading comfort zone. It is through the process of guided reading that students not only learn how to read but learn to love reading.

DOWNLOAD YOUR FREE GIFT BELOW:

Go from Stress to Success with These 15 Powerful Tips

You're in The Tunnel, Now Turn on The Light:

Here are The Best Ways to Transform Your Success

Do You Feel Stressed-Out, Overwhelmed and Harassed Every Day?

Then you're stuck in a negative thought spiral that is keeping you from achieving *real success!*

How many times have you thought, 'if only I could be more productive, then I'd get ahead?' No matter how hard you try, it eludes you. Most people experience intense self-doubt, worry and negative thinking at some point in their careers. These are your immediate obstacles to success.

This guide tackles these issues with easy, direct solutions to help you break the cycle and get back on track. These 15 powerful tips will take you from overwhelmed to overjoyed, in no time!

This FREE Cheat Sheet contains:

- Essential tips on how to stop worrying and start living
- How to actually relieve anxiety and banish it for good
- Ways to get rid of negative thoughts, and how to stop them from recurring
- Tips to become the most productive, motivated version of yourself
- How to focus on career success and build positive cycles and habits

Scroll down and click the link below to Claim your Free Cheat Sheet!

I want you to know that you don't have to live this way. You don't have to feel like these negative cycles are getting the better of you. Your career is waiting to bloom – and flourish! Give yourself the opportunity to make the right choices, by learning how to authentically reach for lasting success.

Ditch the stress, embrace success.

Click Here!

Check out our Other *AMAZING* Titles:

Book 1: Neuro-Linguistic Programming (NLP) Essential Guide

The Best Hacks, Tricks and Techniques for Mastering Neuro-Linguistic Programming

The name "Neuro-linguistic Programming," or NLP, refers to its foundations of the three foremost influencers that govern human experience: these being Neurology, Language, and Programming. The

Neurological system regulates the body's many functions; Language pertains to how we communicate with others and ourselves; and Programming refers to the models and systems in our world: what output should we receive from a given input? NLP illustrates these three underlying forces, and the powerful connection between our mind (Neuro), language (Linguistic), and behavior (Programming).

1.) The map is not the zone.

This can be an initially perplexing idea, but bear with me! "The map is not the zone" professes that no human will ever know reality, as they can only know what they perceive as reality. Humans respond to everything around them through their own personal sensory systems. The feelings and emotions I experience from watching a particular movie will not be the same as those that you experience from watching the same movie. In the same way, two maps of a hiking trail could be quite different from each other, though they both describe the same physical trail. The map is not the trail itself.

Similarly, it is the neuro-linguistic maps of reality that determine how a person behaves and gives that behavior meaning, not reality itself. Generally, it is not the reality that encourages or limits a person, but their own map of reality.

2.) Life and mind are complete procedures.

The various processes that take place both within an individual and between humans and their environment are organized. The human body, society, and the universe form a complete system with sub-systems, all of which interact and influence one another. The models and techniques that form the bases of NLP are a combination of the two principles outlined above. NLP teaches that it is impossible for humans to know objective reality. It, also, teaches that wisdom, ethics, and organization are not found by having the "true" map of the world, since humans are not capable of creating one.

Instead, the goal is to create the richest map possible, respecting the systems that govern ourselves and the world that we inhabit. The most effective people are those who have a map that allows them to perceive the largest number of choices and perspectives. NLP is all about expanding your mind to see new possibilities you haven't even dreamed of. Excellence is derived from having many choices and wisdom comes from various perspectives.

The founders of NLP

The founders of neuro-linguistic programming were John Grinder and Richard Bandler. In the 1970s, their goal was to create explicit models of human excellence. The Structure of Magic was their first collaboration and identified the behavior and verbal patterns of two colleagues, namely Virginia Satir and Fritz Perls. This was soon followed up with Patterns of Hypnotic Techniques of Milton. H. Erickson, which examined the behavior and verbal patterns of Erickson, one of the world's most renowned psychiatrists of all time.

From their early works, Grinder and Bandler formalized their techniques and findings with their individual contributions and called this "Neuro-linguistic Programming." The aim was to symbolize the relationship that was made between the brain, language, and body. Throughout the years, NLP has been refined and has developed further skills and tools for communication and change. NLP is particularly effective in a number of professional areas today, including sales, counseling, law, management, creativity, psychotherapy, health, education, and more.

Since the beginnings of NLP in the mid-70s, the topic has evolved considerably, spread around the world, and touched the lives of many. The 1990s saw a new generation of NLP begin to develop, and this form of NLP focuses on issues such as identity, mission, and vision.

Disassociation

What is disassociation? Well, in NLP, this is a term that defines a wide range of experiences from the mild detachment to immediate surroundings, to severe detachment from emotional and physical experiences. Essentially, dissociation serves as the bridge between the negative state of mind and the cause event. In this case, it is very effective and a long-term remedy for entrenched deeply psychological problems like depression, anxiety, phobias, and stress.

In our day-to-day life, we experience anxiety, stress, and negative emotions. These states of feeling are trigger reactions to common experiences. For example, you may not notice your temper rising when you hear someone discuss a particular 'hot topic,' or even after mentioning a certain word or phrase (a trigger topic, phrase, or action). Fortunately, the power of disassociation in NLP is supreme. It can help you positively deal with difficulties at home, work, or in all your relationships.

Dissociation is one of the most practical tools. Its wrought changes are so real and become manifested in a very short period. Once you combine dissociation with the other four techniques, you will rapidly notice a wide range of positive self-improvements in how you react to objects and people in the universe around you. With that being said, now that you know what dissociation is, aren't you curious to explore some of its benefits and why you should apply it to change your awkward behavior? If you are, here goes…

Benefits of Dissociation

The core benefit of dissociation is to give you the insight to see every situation as an observer and let you evaluate it impartially. Dissociation has proven highly effective against habitual reflexes, phobias, and irrational fears. Dissociation is somewhat a searchlight that clarifies the unthinking or exaggerated behavior and allows you to commence changes free from the influence of powerful emotion and instincts.

Dissociation enables you to have a sense of heartfelt compassion. Through dissociation, you can easily understand another person's perspective, hence experience minimal miscommunications with people around you. Dissociation enables you to have a sense of humility and respect for yourself and others. You want to see your past facades and fakes? Use dissociation!

Easy NLP Disassociation Technique

Are you curious to apply this technique to change your life? Below is a six-point program that uncovers it all. You can easily use these six steps to exercise disassociation and get all the benefits seen above.

Step #1: Recognize the emotional fear you aim to control or get rid of. This can be an irrational fear of cockroaches or a dislike of garlic. Similarly, it can be an unclear uneasiness about a particular place or lack of trust to a particular type of people.

Step #2: In your mind's eye, visualize a situation where you encounter this unwanted emotional experience. Visualize it and feel it deep down as completely as you can. Observe the encounter completely from start to finish, but imagine you are not involved. You are just outside observing this situation from the perspective of a third party. This means you can view yourself and the irrational object, and witness the drama coming from an objective perspective.

Step #3: After you have completed watching the scene from a third person's perspective, rewind it so that the events play in reverse.

Step #4: Again, fast forward through the scenario, having the picture of the events in your mind at double-speed, then replay back to the start again.

Step #5: Introduce an element of creative fun to the visualization. Play your scene backward, but this time use a humorous soundtrack to the creative visualization. It's up to you to choose the kind of music you want, but I would prefer a music hall piano theme relevant to the low-tone comedy movie soundtracks of the early 1820s. Repeat this continuously, both backward and forward.

Step #6: Remove the music and the creative visualization addition to the scene in your mind's eye and replay the scene directly from your perspective, making it as detailed as possible. This time, your emotional response toward the object or situation should be changed or should have disappeared

Keep repeating this practice. In case it fails to work on the first trial, don't lose hope. Your deep relaxed phobias can take many rewinds before you notice an effect, but insistence will reward you.

Book 2: Short Term Memory Improvement

Foolproof Atomic Strategies for Short Term Memory Optimization

There is no such thing as a decent or terrible memory for names; there is just a decent or an awful system. In this part, you will learn methods that can have a huge effect on your name memory.

Make up your mind today to be better; it is a decision that will give you various advantages and spare you from many humiliating circumstances.

Dispose of your restricting beliefs about your name memory and begin to concentrate on finding a system that can help you. Be inspired and keen on names and how we mark individuals as indicated by that name.

Picture in your mind that you meet an individual who says that he will give you a million dollars if you could recall his name seven days from today. Is it possible that you would recollect it? Definitely, with the right kind of motivation, we are all amazing at recalling names.

The techniques that I will impart in you have been in use for quite a long period of time. The following methods require that you think in a new way and effectively engage your associating mind. Some say the system of association to remember names is not effective for them. The truth is, this system does not work if it is not practiced, in fact, nothing in life works unless you put it to work. By employing the association methods, all memory masters can easily remember up to one hundred names under thirty minutes.

The untrained memory is not entirely dependable. An average individual gambles with his memory, leaving it to chance and hoping that the name will somehow stick. The following strategies to which you will be exposed are effective- make use of them!

To recall names, focus on the four C's below:

1. Concentrate

When you meet somebody with the same name as yours, do you recall their name? Of course! This is due to the fact that the name interests you, you hear it often, and your attention is at a peak. The name has significance to you and also, you associate the name to yourself. In the event that you are able to maintain this essential strategy with each individual that you meet you will recollect their names.

At the time when we are introduced to people, they ordinarily state their name so fast that no one can catch it. Take charge of the introduction. If truly you are going to get the name, you have to make the introduction go slowly. Put your elephant ears on and truly hear the name, make recalling names a thing that is dear to you.

Oliver Wendel Holmes said, "A person must get a thing before they can forget it." It is important that you hear the name well first because if you don't hear something, it is impossible to recall it. First, catch the name so as to be able to transform it into a memory. You will improve your remembrance if you not only hear the name but also say it back to the individual. Ask the individual to repeat their names in instances where you did not hear the name, and if it is not an easy name, ask the person to spell the name out to you.

Be attentive and take a genuine interest in the other individual's name. Often times we are stressing about being interesting, that we neglect to be interested. You will take more interest in listening to the name when you are more interested. Make an effort to listen to people from their point of view and not yours. This will enhance your name memory as well as social intelligence.

2. Create

It is important that you make a picture for the name in your head, so that you may be able to re-create it later.

Have you at any point heard individuals state, "I know the face; however, I can't recall the name...?" You never hear individuals state, "The face is on the tip of my tongue." We recollect faces since they create a picture in our mind. The names don't ordinarily 'stick' since we make an effort to recall it with our sound-related memory or our little voice. It is silly to try to attach a sound to a mental picture – it would definitely not stick. In addition, sound-related memories are never as strong as visual memories.

To make a memory stick, it is essential that we make a picture out of the name. Recall how we created pictures out of names when memorizing the first twelve presidents? When you give a name meaning, you would then be able to recall it.

If you put a name in your mind and do nothing with it, it will fade away, and you will be unable to recall it again. This is on the grounds that working memory doesn't save data. Therefore, to store it you will need help from your short-term and long-term memory. You need to truly think about the name to recollect it since we usually recall what we think about.

When you meet with somebody, you have about twenty seconds to think of the name and make a connection. Should you not do anything with the name in twenty seconds, the name will disappear from memory. The more associations and significance you can give the name, the more it will 'stick.'

Some names will normally make an image like the last names Baker, Cruise or Gardner. Other names might be some trouble, however by using a touch of imagination any name can be given significance and transformed into an image.

3. Connect

Keep in mind that all learning is making a connection between what is known and what is not. You will definitely know the face; all you are left to do is to link the strange name to the familiar face. When you see the face, it must operate as a trigger or peg to bring the name to your consciousness.

Below are a few strategies to make the connection. Every one of the techniques you learn here takes significantly longer to describe than to use.

Comparison Connection. With this strategy, you associate the individual to a name that you definitely know. Suppose we meet an individual by the name of George. To make the name recall, we consider somebody that we definitely know with a similar name. Do you know another George? You may even consider a celebrity with a similar name, such as George Clooney.

After this, all we are left to do in our mind is to put the two individuals side by side. What shade of hair does the George that we are meeting have? What shade is the other George's hair? By carefully considering this characteristic, you would be more attentive than before, as such making a more grounded connection.

Make comparison using various characteristics, and you will concentrate thereby making a long-lasting impression for accurate remembrance. It is as straightforward as that—simply make a comparison between the two faces, and you will recall them. Impact your memory more by picturing the individual with two heads – theirs, and that of the individual you definitely know with a similar name.

I like this strategy since it encourages you not only to recollect the new individual but also to reinforce the other name as well. This strategy takes just a couple of seconds to enable you never to forget the individual's name. We are making use of the memory rule of employing a long-term name and utilizing it to recall the short-term new name.

A few people ask, what occurs in the event that you don't have a name that is similar to compare it with? In this case, we may use other techniques that I will describe to you now. Discover the method that works best for you.

Face Connection. With this strategy, you make a connection between the name and a remarkable characteristic on the individual's face. Each individual's face is one of a kind, and each face has an extraordinary characteristic. For instance, picture that you meet with a lady and the principal thing that strikes you about her face is that she has remarkable blue eyes. At that point, that becomes her exceptional characteristic. When she does tell you her name, you will have a spot to put the name. Assume she says her name is Janice. At that point, you make a picture of the name: Janice sounds like chain ice. Next, you make the association and think about a chain of ice escaping from her blue eyes.

Here is another instance, picture that you meet a man and you see that he has a huge nose and his name is Peter. Transform the name into an image; you would then be able to picture a 'Pea eater.' Next, make a quick association that the man's nose is a big pea eater. By creating a silly but brilliant connection, you will be able to link the face and the name together.

Using this strategy, do not tell anyone what you have done in your head. It is private, and a few people may end up insulted. I once met a woman whose name is Hazel. She asked me how I was able to recall her name, and I made a huge mistake of telling her. I told her I thought of the nut, hazelnut. She definitely was not impressed by this.

Keep in mind that a large number of individuals like to identify with their names. They think of it as their own exceptional brand. If you make fun of the name, you're in turn making fun of them.

A couple of questions that people ask about this strategy are:

What do I do if I meet four individuals and every one of them has a remarkable nose?

Looking for the extraordinary characteristic encourages you to concentrate on the face in such a way that you may never have done before. A lot of people do not truly take in the appearance of a person when they are meeting them. So, the feature is majorly about concentrating on the face and making a connection. I have demonstrated this technique before by recalling more than one hundred names in thirty minutes. When you meet a hundred people, you make use of a considerable number of similar characteristics; however, there will never be any confusion. You can rehearse this technique on Facebook since there are a large number of appearances to look over.

Is it possible that I connect the name of a person to the clothes?

Of course, however, this is only if you take note of the individual's face as well. Each person's face does not change much because it is unique, but in the case of clothes, people change outfits.

What occurs in the event that it's hard for me to form a mental image of the individual's name?

You can picture scribbling their name on their forehead. Ensure you make use of a gigantic red mental pen. It is about being creative. If you create their name in your head, you will recollect the name with as much effortlessness as you recall the face.

Meeting Location Connection. The first time we meet people, we are likely to recall where we initially met them. The place establishes an unmistakable connection in our memory; however, the name is absent!

With this strategy, we link the name to where we met the individual. We are making use of a journey peg to hang on to the name. Suppose we meet a lady that bears the name Rose. You should ask yourself, "What will I recall about this place where I meet her?" Let's say you figure you will recollect the buffet table; next, you associate a big rose that's red in color to it and anytime you think about the place her name will come to you.

4. Continuous Use

Should you focus and get the name, make it significant and associate it to the individual, and this will help you to recall the name for the short-term period. In any case, to make the name stick in your memory always, you need to keep on making use of it.

Discuss the name. In the event that it is a foreign name, ask the individual what it stands for. How would you spell it? Likewise, use the name while discussing. If you talk about the name continuously, you will depend less on working memory, and you will start to save it.

In your head, ask yourself, "What is that individual's name again?" Get the appropriate response and afterward ask yourself, "Does that feel right?" Try to make the connection stronger over the length of the day or night.

Look over the name. Make a section for names in your journal, on your personal computer or on your cell phone of individuals that you might want to recall. Welcome individuals you would like to remember to one of your social networking sites, with the goal of reviewing their names. Do a review of the names regularly so as to store these names in your long-term memory. It's only an issue of scribbling the name down with a pen and the location where you met the individual. Take a look at the list every once in a while, and you will have a large name memory documenting system; it will be impossible to be unaware of a name again.

These techniques can be used to recall several individuals at one gathering. They are altogether intended to enhance your focus because when you remember others, they also make an effort to remember you.

Book 3: Best Way to Stop Procrastination Fast

Secret Techniques to Get Things Done, Increase Productivity and Kill the Inner Procrastinator

Time management is often said to be the "secret" of successful and productive people. In theory, it sounds like an excellent idea, but time management is harder to achieve than most people think. Like most of the concerns in this book, time management makes use of your willpower to follow through with the plans you've put on paper.

Plan, Execute, Assess, Repeat

There are essentially four steps in time management: (1) the plan, (2) the execution, (3) the assessment of what you've done, and (4) the repetition. Most people are stuck with number 2, and even if they make it all the way to number 3, the fourth part is where they usually stumble. Take a good look at your time management loop and figure out which part you usually have a problem with and address it accordingly.

Planning Stage

The planning stage is where most people dwell when attempting time management. There's nothing quite like the enjoyment of planning your future actions on paper as it looks good in theory. You tell yourself you'll finish something within a specified time frame when in reality, it's going to take you twice that time to make a difference. The mere act of "promising" yourself of success makes you happy, but are you following through with these promises?

While the planning stage is not as important as the execution stage, it does help with the overall scheme of things. Planning stage encompasses not just what you should be doing and what time you should be doing it but also what should be done if you become distracted from what you're supposed to do. Anti-distraction techniques are discussed in a different portion of this book. Try to apply any of those techniques mentioned and incorporate them into your planning stage.

Execution Stage

This is the point where most people have a problem. An efficient time management system should make it easier for you to execute the plans you have. Techniques discussed in this book may also be applied in this portion of the activity. Unfortunately, it all falls to willpower and self-discipline on the part of the individual.

Evaluation Stage

The evaluation stage is an important aspect of the time management process. It's essentially the stage where you confront reality and realize whether your methods work or not. What techniques work for you and which ones do not? Ideally, you should be able to evaluate each one and figure out whether you should continue with this particular technique or use a different one.

Essential Principles of a Time Management System

Time management systems (TMS) are incredibly flexible and customizable, which is why they may vary from one person to the next. The methods you use may be largely different from the methods used by another person. Hence, there's no set formula other than the plan-execute-evaluate-repeat method.

When creating a time management system for your personal use, however, there are some principles that you should adhere to for it to be effective and easily followed. Here are some of those principles to keep in mind:

It Must Be Simple

Simplicity encompasses a straightforward approach to time management. It shouldn't leave you guessing as to what you should do and how you should do it—in theory, simple answers to two questions: "What should be done?" and "When should it be done?"

Hence, the most basic approach is by simply grabbing your daily planner and jotting down the activity you need to do on a particular day. The complexity arises when you have a hard time performing the task due to a variety of reasons such as (1) you don't know how to start, (2) there are too many items that need to be addressed, or even (3) you're just too lazy to get started.

Once these roadblocks start to appear, simplicity tends to go out the window, requiring you to be a bit more creative with your approach to time management. Hence, instead of simply sitting down and starting on the task, you'll have first to eliminate the distractions or even move completely to a different place to maintain your focus.

A time management system, therefore, starts simple and then branches off into more complex conditions when you're just starting to enforce or instill the habit. As a beginner, you might find yourself suffering from false starts and stops as you encourage yourself into following through with the "simple" layout. As you get used to the habit, however, and as your self-discipline develops, the TMS can become simpler with no need to provide for extraordinary instances.

It Must Be Complete

Completion talks of taking into consideration everything that needs to be done in relation to the primary goal. For example, you need to write a paper for one of your classes. The completion of the paper is the primary goal, but there are sub-goals under this. An example would be the need to figure out the theme of a paper, the research studies you'll need to use for information, and how the information will be presented on paper. If you constantly "refer back" to different materials while writing the paper, then this will equate to time wasted as you switch from one particular task to another.

Hence, it's crucial that the subtasks have been completed before the primary task is tackled. By doing so, you'll have everything you need on hand before proceeding to the primary goal. Simply put, you need to make sure you have all the ingredients in the kitchen before you proceed with cooking. Otherwise, you might find yourself having to run to the grocery store to grab eggs, milk, and other vital ingredients.

It Must Be Connected

The connection is largely related to completeness. In the above example, you need to be complete in your sub-goals before going after the primary goal. Note though that it's not enough that you have all the ingredients on hand. Connection takes into account the establishment of order in how you do things. What must be tackled first? What items can be delayed? Which ones are considered the prerequisite of a later task?

It Must Be Realistic

Of course, don't forget the requirement that your goals must be realistic. They must be doable within the time frame that you've allowed yourself; otherwise, you'd be demanding too much and never actually finish or accomplish the task you've set.

Ways of Setting Priorities

One important aspect of time management systems is the setting or deciding on priorities. This is primarily entrenched in the planning stage and can be approached in several ways. Following are just some of the methods you can use:

ABC Analysis

This method of prioritizing tasks is often used in businesses for handling large quantities of data. Each group is marked as A, B, or C with corresponding categories. For example, *A tasks* are those that are urgent and important. *B tasks* are those that are important but not urgent, and the *C tasks* are not important. Further classifications can be done, but for the most part, these are the basic groups in which tasks are made. In some cases, companies force-rank the tasks within the B group to either A or C to create a clearer picture of how and when it should be done.

This kind of priority assessment is best used when it comes to household chores or when you have to work on several projects all at once. In many cases, you might find yourself shifting the tasks around as time moves along. For example, the unimportant might suddenly become urgent and important as the specific date approaches. Those that fall within the B category might be promoted to the A category as the tasks in the A category decreases.

Pareto Analysis

The Pareto analysis is often used in conjunction with the ABC analysis. This method is a little confusing at first, but once mastered, it is quite straightforward. The general principle of this technique is that 80 percent of your tasks can be completed in just 20 percent of your disposable time. Consequently, 20 percent of the tasks will consume roughly 80 percent of your time.

The Pareto analysis compels you to categorize activities in just two parts. Those that can be finished within 20 percent of your disposable time should be assigned a higher priority compared to the latter.

The Pareto analysis also takes into consideration the possibility of performing a task simply. This means finding alternative methods to shorten the amount of time you devote to a task without having to compromise on quality.

Compared to the ABC analysis, the Pareto analysis (also known as the 80-20 rule) is a bit more confusing. How exactly will you apply this to everyday life?

One thing you have to bear in mind is that the Pareto analysis is used to narrow down on the problems and resolve a solution by figuring out the possible causes or obstruction in accomplishing the task. Here's how the Pareto analysis is usually applied:

1. A person starts by identifying the problems that require a solution.

2. The root cause of each problem must be identified. You can try writing down several root causes.

3. The next step is to score each problem based on actual and measurable data. For example, your problem is about finding out just how frequently customers return products. You score it based on the number of times returns occur. If the problem is about spending too much money on a business, you can score it based on the money equivalent.

4. Due to possible variances in the scoring system, it's perfectly possible to use a common scoring system, like a scale of 1 to 5. However, you can also use a common scoring system by grouping the problems based on measurable data. For example, you're spending too much money on marketing, on repairs, on electric bills, and food. All these can be grouped, and the cost in dollars can be used to "score" each one based on the amount

you're spending in excess.

5. Once you're done scoring each problem, take a good look at the root causes of each problem. This is the important step: group the problems according to the root cause. For example, if problems 2, 5, and 8 have the same X root cause, you'll have to group them.

6. Once you've grouped the problems according to their common root cause, the next step is to add the scores of the newly grouped problems. The highest sum would take top priority; the second highest would take second priority and so on.

7. At this stage, what you have are separate problem groups having the same root cause. This is where the 80-20 rule becomes more obvious. By creating a solution that addresses a single root cause, you'll be able to essentially "solve" all the problems within that group.

You'll find that the Pareto analysis is available through Excel.

Eisenhower Method

The Eisenhower method is named so because it was rumored to be the organization technique utilized by Dwight Eisenhower. He's also the one who uttered the famous quote: "I have two kinds of problem, the urgent and the important. The urgent is not important, and the important is never urgent."

The Eisenhower method, therefore, makes use of these criteria when grouping or prioritizing tasks. There are essentially four quadrants.

The Super Reader Protocol

1. First is the "important and urgent" quadrant, which includes tasks that need to be done quickly, immediately, and personally.

2. Next is the "important and not urgent" quadrant, which usually involves recreational stuff or the planning of activities in the not-so-distant future.

3. There's also the "unimportant but urgent" quadrant, which can include interruptions or meetings that are not factored in the grand scheme of things but getting them done quickly helps clear up all the things you have to do.

4. Last would be the "not important and not urgent" quadrant. Items falling within this quadrant are typically dropped or delayed until the other quadrants are empty. They're typically time-wasting activities, such as checking your Facebook or reading a book for pleasure.

References

Alison (2016, March). How to craft a strong book introduction for guided reading. Retrieved from https://learningattheprimarypond.com/blog/book-introduction-guided-reading/

Alison. (2018, June). What does a pre-A guided reading lesson look like? Retrieved from https://learningattheprimarypond.com/blog/what-does-a-pre-a-guided-reading-lesson-look-like/

Alphakids Assessment Kit. (2002). How to take running records. Retrieved from http://scholastic.ca/education/movingupwithliteracyplace/pdfs/grade4/runningrecords.pdf

Bainbridge, C. (2019, October). Top 5 skills needed for childhood literacy. Retrieved from https://www.verywellfamily.com/literacy-skills-1449194

BenchMark Education (n.d.). Guided reading activities and small-group instruction. Retrieved from https://benchmarkeducation.com/best-practices-library/read-about-best-practices-in-small-group-instruction.html

Bookroo (n.d.). The 100 best quotes about guided reading. Retrieved from https://bookroo.com/blog/the-100-best-quotes-about-reading

Doman, M. (2012, November). A parent's guide to guided reading. Retrieved from https://www.scholastic.com/parents/books-and-reading/reading-resources/book-selection-tips/parents-guide-to-guided-reading.html

Fountas, I. & Pinnell, G. S. (2018, July). Teachers tip: Selecting books for guided reading. Retrieved from https://fpblog.fountasandpinnell.com/teacher-tip-selecting-books-for-guided-reading.

Fountas & Pinnell Literacy. (n.d.). 5 Steps to preparing an introduction to a text for guided reading lessons: a teacher's tip. Retrieved from https://fpblog.fountasandpinnell.com/5-steps-to-preparing-an-introduction-to-a-text-for-guided-reading-lessons-a-teacher-tip-from-fountas-and-pinnell

Fountas & Pinnell Literacy. (n.d.). Leveled literacy intervention (LLI), Retrieved from https://www.fountasandpinnell.com/lli/

G, A. (2018, January). An overview of the guided reading levels. Retrieved from https://www.themeasuredmom.com/overview-of-guided-reading-levels/

Hargreaves, A. (2018, January.) Great quotes about reading and the reading life. Retrieved from https://bookriot.com/2018/01/12/quotes-about-reading/

Literacy Footprints (n.d.). Literacy footprints: A research-based guided reading system. Retrieved from https://www.literacyfootprints.com/literacy-footprints-a-research-based-guided-reading-system

McLeod, S. (2019). The zone of proximal development and scaffolding. Retrieved from https://www.simplypsychology.org/Zone-of-Proximal-Development.html

Michael, (n.d.). How to organize your reading groups. Retrieved from https://www.thethinkerbuilder.com/2015/07/how-to-organize-your-small-groups-to.html

Reading A-Z (n.d.). Stages of development. Retrieved from https://www.readinga-z.com/learninga-z-levels/stages-of-development/

Zuniga, L. (n.d.). Develop independence with guided reading. Retrieved from https://www.learninga-z.com/site/breakroom/guided-reading-independence

www.ingramcontent.com/pod-product-compliance
Lightning Source LLC
Chambersburg PA
CBHW050001230526
45465CB00003BB/1202